LIVING LARGE

LIVING LARGE

A Big Man's Ideas on Weight, Success, and Acceptance

Michael S. Berman with Laurence Shames

RODALE

Alameda Free Library
1550 Oak Street
Alameda, CA 94501

Book design by Drew Frantzen

Library of Congress Cataloging-in-Publication Data

Berman, Michael S.
  Living large : a big man's ideas on weight, success, and acceptance / Michael S. Berman ; with Laurence Shames.
      p.   cm.
    ISBN-13 978–1–59486–277–9 hardcover
    ISBN-10 1–59486–277–X hardcover
    1. Berman, Michael S.—Health.   2. Overweight men—United States—Biography.   I. Shames, Laurence.   II. Title.
  RC552.O25B49   2006
  362.196'3980092—dc22   2005031222

Distributed to the trade by Holtzbrinck Publishers

2   4   6   8   10   9   7   5   3   1   hardcover

To Carol—

my friend, my partner, my love—who more than anyone has borne the burden of my fatness.

CONTENTS

Part 3: Some Things I've Learned

My name is Mike Berman. I'm 66 years old, five feet nine inches tall, and I weigh 235 pounds. Today, that is. Over the course of my adult life, I've weighed as much as 332 and as little as 217. I've spent years commuting between 230 and 280; I've crossed the 300-pound threshold four or five times. I would reckon, conservatively, that when all my ups and downs are figured in, I have gained and lost well over a thousand pounds—more than three times my total weight, even at my heaviest.

In short, I am a fat man. But I am also a happy man. Yes, those two things can go together—though it took me a lot of years, a lot of pain, and a lot of psychotherapy to realize that.

Along the way I realized something else as well: that my best chance for peace of mind and also for controlling my weight lay in *accepting* my situation. I don't mean giving up on the hope of being thinner; I have always tried to lose more weight, and I always will. I mean being honest and realistic about what I'm up against. I've accepted the hard but liberating notion that I have a disease. My fatness is not a function of "willpower" or "discipline" or "laziness" or "weakness." It's the result of physical and psychological factors that are outside of my control. Like diabetes or flat feet, my fatness is a chronic malady that can't be cured but *can* be managed.

Let me make it clear that having a disease is no excuse to shirk responsibility. I have a problem, but I am not helpless. I don't see myself as a victim. I refuse to be passive or self-pitying when it comes to my well-being. Every life has its difficulties, and being fat is one of mine. That's just how it is. Still, I have a choice—a choice made far tougher and more complicated by my disease, but a choice nonetheless—as to whether or not I eat that piece of chocolate, whether or not I keep my appointment with the treadmill.

But responsibility is one thing; guilt is something else. Responsibility is positive, a duty we owe to ourselves, a matter of self-respect. Guilt is destructive. Guilt breeds desperation—and desperation makes it even harder to make good decisions.

In recent years—after more than six decades of living as a fat person—I have finally learned to stop feeling guilty and desperate about my weight. Again, this doesn't mean I am thrilled to be fat or that I've stopped working at becoming thinner. But I have largely moved beyond the torment. The pressure is off. I don't *have* to lose weight; I'm okay the way I am.

Needless to say, this acceptance has made me a much happier and less frustrated person. But it has had another, completely unexpected bonus as well. I have found that since I don't *have* to lose weight, I *can* lose weight—and keep it off more successfully than ever before. These days I hardly ever binge, and if I do overindulge, it's likely to be with healthy foods. I seem finally to have tamed the wild fluctuations of weight that have plagued me all my life. I am in control of my fatness, rather than being controlled by it—and I am proud of this. To me, at least, it feels like a victory.

This book is the story of the gradual, often agonizing, and unsteady progress by which I have learned to manage my weight effectively and to live a full and satisfying life in spite of having the fat disease. I am not writing as an "expert"; I am not a doctor, a scientist, or a therapist, and I have no ambition to set up shop as a diet guru. I claim no credentials other than the life that I have lived.

As a fat boy I was assaulted with taunts and name-calling. As an adolescent I endured the loneliness of living at the social margin, and as a young man I learned the anguish of the blind date, that awful moment when the woman you are meeting quite literally *sizes you up* and decides, before you've said a word, that you are not the man of her dreams. Even in my professional life, I have felt the need to work harder, prepare more thoroughly—to be *better*—in order to neutralize the antifat bias of others.

I've been on probably 20 different diets—Weight Watchers, Stillman, Pritikin, Scarsdale, Atkins, South Beach, you name it—in several cases more than once. On three occasions I've entered residential weight-loss programs. I've been hospitalized to go on fasts that permitted only water, vitamins, and minerals; starved for 10 days, I have had the bizarre experience of hallucinating giant cheeseburgers.

In past decades I have had a closetful of clothes with waist sizes ranging from 44 to 58; I hated to throw any of them away, because I never knew when I might be that size again. All in all, I know what it is to live life as a fat person.

I know, as well, how difficult it is to get straightforward, trustworthy advice about the realities of managing fatness. Oh, there's plenty of information out there. *Too much* information, most of it written by people who are not fat themselves, who don't know how life *feels* inside the body of a fat person, and who are trying to make money from our desperate desire to be thin. Much of the "information" from these sources turns out to consist of false promises, phony hope, half-truths, and dubious claims that are then *dis*claimed by the tiny print at the bottom of the label. An ever-expanding weight-loss industry tries to sell us this diet or that pill or some brand-new miracle supplement. But isn't it obvious that if the pills and diets really worked, if the quick fixes delivered what they promised, the weight-loss business would be *shrinking*, not growing?

If you are reading these pages, chances are that you, like me, are afflicted with the fat disease—or you care about a fat person who is important in your life as spouse, partner, friend, or colleague. I believe this book will help you, that my story will ring true for you. People are more alike than different, and my hunch is that many fat people have felt what I have felt—have experienced the shame, frustration, and disappointments I have known—and can learn to more effectively manage both their weight and their feelings, as I have.

If, like mine, your relationship with food is a charged one—if you look to food not only for nourishment and pleasure but for solace and reward; if you sneak food or lie to yourself or others about your eating; if your weight tends to yo-yo, whether the range is 20 pounds or a hundred; if you've felt mystified and defeated by your inability to keep off weight that you've worked so hard to lose—then chances are your situation, like mine, is a chronic one. You have a condition without a once-and-final cure.

That may seem like a pessimistic statement, but in fact it's just the opposite. Chronic diseases are the ones that don't destroy you! They can be understood, tamed, and kept under control. But the work of management must be ongoing and must come from within. There *are* answers, but you won't find them in some trendy diet book. There *are* techniques that work, but they go way beyond the latest fitness regimen or diet supplement or pill. You *can* be thinner—but if you want to *stay* thinner, a single dramatic episode of weight loss probably won't take you where you want to go; you need a long-term strategy that addresses not just what you eat but who you are.

I have labored for many years to evolve a strategy that works for me. I hope this book will provide help and comfort and reassurance as you move toward a strategy of acceptance and management that will work for you.

I started making jottings for this volume way back in 1997. When I was ready to write a proposal, I showed some pages to a trusted friend familiar with the realities of publishing. Although he was intrigued by the material, he urged me not to go public with my story, for fear that it would compromise my dignity. His opinion, motivated by kindness and caring, gave me pause. But on reflection I found that I could not agree.

It is not undignified to be fat. It is not undignified to tell the truth—to admit one's failings and acknowledge one's pain. It's the things we don't talk about that haunt us.

That being so, I have been struck—and bothered—that, for all the torrent of talk and writing about obesity in our society, relatively little discussion has been carried forward by fat people themselves, especially fat men. Why? Is there some perverse taboo dictating that thin people can talk about fat, can preach and scold, but fat people must keep quiet? I can only assume that most fat men have been silent because of embarrassment, shyness, or shame; or maybe weight is just one of those things that men don't talk about. I would be gratified if I could help to change that.

Other friends of mine, people who know me very well, had reactions to this manuscript that really flabbergasted me. Even my wife, Carol, seemed genuinely surprised at how much distress my story conveyed. What people said, in essence, was, "Mike, we hardly recognize the person in this book. This is sad. This is tormented. This is *not you!*"

Well, it *is* me . . . or one side of me, at least. Like many fat people, I have lived a kind of double life. Viewed from the outside, I am reasonably cheerful, sociable, effective; viewed from within, I have been prey to anguish and frustrations that I generally kept hidden even from my friends. In this book I hope to bring those dark places out into the daylight, both as a catharsis for myself and, I hope, a validation for others who have felt those bleak emotions and been hesitant to share them.

But I don't want to overplay the dark side of my story because the truth is that, fat or no fat, I am basically a happy person. I don't mean happy with the false gaiety of the "jolly fat man," and I certainly don't mean happy all the time. The things that bother most people—rudeness, job stress, traffic jams—bother me too. But all in all I have been blessed with a wonderful life. I've been married to a terrific and accomplished woman for more than 40 years. I've met with success in a career I find extremely gratifying. I have a circle of great friends whom I cherish. I have discovered—somewhat to my own surprise—that fatness does not rule out confidence or romance, nor is it an excuse for holding back from the richness and variety of experience.

Over the decades, I have worked my way toward a simple but, I believe, important understanding that is at the heart of everything I have to say:

It is not the goal of life to be thin. It is the goal of life to be happy.

Again, those two goals are not in conflict. They both become more attainable as you stop beating yourself up for being fat and accept your fatness as a condition to be managed, a challenge to be faced.

Not that acceptance comes easily or magically does away with the difficulties of being seriously overweight. I struggle every single day to control my eating. I'm still a fat person; I'm still preoccupied with being fat. And this would be so even if, by some miracle, I awoke tomorrow morning and weighed 170. It's not about the numbers; it's about who I am.

I still count calories—in fact, I enter my caloric intake in a notebook every day, along with the number of minutes I exercise. I'm resigned to the fact that my preoccupation—some might say compulsion—will never go away. Just as a recovering alcoholic is still an alcoholic, a fat person with some hard-won insight is still a fat person.

What I've gained by accepting my fatness, however, is this: When I get on the scale, I understand that I'm weighing only my body—not my self-worth, not the value of my life. I've learned that the scale is only a mechanical device, not an altar for the sacrifice of my self-respect or my contentment.

Would I rather be a thin person? You know, until quite recently I would have regarded that question as a real no-brainer. Of course I'd rather be thinner! Wouldn't everybody?

Now I see the question as being far more complicated. Look, being fat is not for wimps. It makes life harder, in ways both trivial and serious. My heart has extra work to do with every beat. I'm not as mobile as I'd like to be. My knees and ankles often hurt. I'm uncomfortable in airplane seats and at the theater. I sometimes see unease and disapproval in the eyes of strangers.

At the same time, being fat has made me who I am. Having a shape that our society labels unattractive has forced me to emphasize other resources—concentration, competence, humor. Having a fat person's sensitivity to slights and biases has, I believe, made me more aware of the feelings of others and equipped me, I hope, to be a caring friend and a responsive husband. The everyday stresses, both physical and social, of living life as a fat person have given me a kind of strength that comes only from quiet struggle.

Being fat, then, like nearly everything else in life, is what you make of it.

PART 1

GROWING UP
AND GROWING FAT

CHAPTER 1

THE BOY WITH BREASTS

In the life of every fat person there is probably some unforgettable moment when one is forced to realize that, in the eyes of the world, one is fat. Not chubby or husky; not pleasingly plump; not even obese. Fat.

Fat becomes the adjective by which one is most easily described. *Fat* becomes the characteristic by which one is most easily identified and distinguished—set apart—from others.

For me, this moment came when I was 13 years old, in the locker room of my junior high school, after gym class. I already hated gym. I was the fattest kid in my group; I saw myself as being slow, weak, and bad at sports. I couldn't climb ropes, couldn't do good pushups. Painfully self-conscious, I dreaded being naked in the shower with the other boys. Probably a lot of us were insecure about our bodies and the baffling changes taking place on the cusp of adolescence, but many other kids masked their discomfort with horseplay and somewhat forced high spirits. I tended toward a different extreme. I hid as much as possible, showered as quickly as I could, and pulled a shirt on even before my skin was fully dry.

On this particular day, the usual group of boys was standing in the long gang-shower, soaping up and joking around. Suddenly, a kid standing next to me made a grab at my soft white chest. He wanted, he said, to know what it was like to feel a girl's breast.

I knocked his hand away and turned my back. The whole thing happened very quickly, and I'm not sure that anyone else even noticed. Still, it was humiliating. Being 13 was difficult enough without being called girlish because of my weight. I rinsed off quickly and got out of there.

That day was the beginning of a long career of using any excuse to avoid gym class. Avoiding exercise, of course, only made me weaker, but at least it spared me the discomfort of taking my shirt off in front of other kids.

If that incident sticks in my mind with special vividness, it was hardly the first time I realized I had an issue with weight or that my relationship with food was passionate but troubled—and had been for about as long as I could remember. A case could be made that I was fat and an overeater from the day I was born.

At birth, I weighed 8 pounds, 13 ounces. Apparently I had a prodigious appetite from the start; in later years my mother joked that I fed so aggressively it hurt her nipples. I was given both breast milk and a supplement. But, hungry though I was, I was often given more food than I really wanted. I was fed even after spitting up. It seems to me that a baby spits up food because he's full, but the thinking at the time was that a baby should be fed until food stays down.

Then there were the starving children of Europe. I was born in 1939; my early childhood corresponded to World War II, and by some peculiar logic it was suggested that chubby children like me could ease suffering around the globe by finishing every last morsel on their plates. Plus, my parents had lived through the Depression. They knew scarcity and insecurity. So they kept the house stocked with food—wonderful food! Corned beef, smoked fish, chopped liver from the deli. Danish, coffee rings, cheesecakes from the bakery. Not to mention the things my mother cooked—briskets, lamb chops, plump and browned roast chickens. My mother took pride and pleasure in her cooking; what better way to show my appreciation than by eating a lot of what she prepared, by asking for seconds no matter how generous my first helping had been?

In retrospect, my parents made mistakes. I don't blame them. Parents are human, and humans do their best with the limited understanding they have. But I was almost certainly fed too much. Our diet was far too heavy in meat and fat and sugar. And our life together as a family was defined first and foremost by meals; I don't think it occurred to any of us that it could be otherwise. Did we go on hikes together? No. Did we exercise together? No. We *ate* together.

Actually, we were probably typical of most middle-class families of the time, yet most members of those families did not become obese. Neither did the rest of my family. My parents were both of normal weight, tending toward the thin side. My two younger sisters were lean kids who grew into slender adults. We all ate at the same table. We all had access to the same cupboards and the same refrigerator. Among my immediate family, I alone am fat. How did it happen?

This question leads to some things that, until recently, I would have found impossible to talk about; even now, it isn't easy. But my intuition tells me that many people harbor secrets similar to mine and would benefit by being unburdened of them. So I will say these things as straightforwardly as I can.

Before I was 5 years old, I was already sneaking food. My first sister had recently been born. To accommodate the baby, my parents moved me to a smaller bedroom—originally a butler's pantry, though we were hardly the sort of family that had a butler—which happened to adjoin the kitchen. Late at night, the apartment dark, the family asleep, I would slip out of bed to raid the refrigerator or the shelves. Cookies, crackers, leftovers—I ate measured amounts of whatever I could forage, always careful to leave enough that my thefts would not be detected. Did my mother notice that half a bag of cookies had become a quarter bag? That a sleeve of saltines was partly gone? That a chicken leg was missing? I really can't say, but I know I was only seldom confronted about it.

By the early years of grade school, certain lifelong patterns seemed already set. I was physically rather sluggish. I didn't run if I could walk; I didn't walk if I could ride. I took little interest in sports, and on the occasions when I tried to get involved, the result was generally disastrous. I was the last kid picked, the one the others groaned about having on the team.

My teachers liked me because I was well-behaved and eager to please. My classmates tended not to like me because I was fat, unathletic, and a favorite of the teachers. I avoided the playground whenever possible because I was already being teased and bullied about my weight. When I couldn't avoid being around groups of other kids, I sought the comfort of an ally and protector. I had one pal—his name was James—who stuck with me and helped keep the bullies away. James was something of a mystery to me. He was fat, though not as fat as I was. Yet he had a physical confidence that I lacked, even a certain swagger; I admired this and knew that I couldn't imitate it.

Inevitably, there were times when the teasers and the bullies caught me alone and I had no choice but to defend myself. Sometimes I'd use my greater size to knock kids down and stomp them. But I didn't like to fight, and though I was bigger than almost all of my contemporaries, I didn't feel that I was strong. Besides, what I wanted was to be liked—or at least left alone. So I evolved a stratagem: In the second or third grade I started bribing kids with candy.

To do this, I had to steal small change from my father's

pockets or my mother's purse. When I'd accumulated 50 cents or a dollar—which bought a lot of candy in those days—I'd go to the store and stock up on Mars bars, Milky Ways, and caramels, which I would then distribute to my tormentors. It never occurred to me to bribe them with, say, comic books or just give them the nickels and dimes directly. No, it had to be food. I guess I believed that only food could work the magic; only food had the power to appease. And of course I didn't give away *all* the candy; I ate a fair percentage of it myself.

When I was 9 years old, my family moved to a house in a different part of Duluth, Minnesota, our town. I changed schools, which made my life a little easier; for some reason, my new classmates made less of an issue of my size. On the home front, though, things were getting more complicated.

My parents, especially my mother, were beginning to see my heaviness as a problem. Because of this, family customs that I'd come to take for granted were suddenly stood on their head. No longer was I served heaping portions and given smiles of approval when I cleaned my plate. No longer was I urged to have seconds. Suddenly I felt that my mother was watching every mouthful I took in; sometimes she was openly critical if I ate too much. At the same time, she still wanted her cooking to be appreciated and enjoyed—a confusing situation, to say the least.

To avoid being criticized, I forced myself to be quite restrained at mealtimes. I took modest portions and sometimes made a rather showy point of leaving something on my plate. But at the same time I was developing yet another ploy so that I could continue to have the extra food I craved.

In our new house, my bedroom wasn't even on the same floor as the kitchen; it was no longer easy to scavenge food in the middle of the night. So I began to stockpile goodies in various hiding places in my room. A package of cupcakes fit easily behind a bookcase. Several bananas could be buried under a pile of socks. My mother was not above searching my room from time to time, and I had to move my stashes often. The more fragrant the foods, the harder they were to conceal. A packaged pie, for instance, could be hidden almost anywhere; a hunk of salami was quite another matter.

Truthfully, I'm not sure if my stashes ever *were* concealed, if in fact I was fooling anybody. Nor can I say with any certainty whether, at some level, I wanted to be caught or if, in the grip of my eating frenzy, I simply didn't care. All I know is that my desire for the food was stronger than anything that might prevent my having it—even shame.

One day I was caught red-handed, in a somewhat macabre way. In a drawer of my nightstand, my mother discovered the head, skin, and skeleton of a smoked fish I had secreted away and eaten. Oily, smelly, and accusing, the ravaged remains should have embarrassed me—and I guess they did. But the embarrassment, far from "curing" my compulsion, only contributed to making it stronger.

Those are some of the basic facts of how I got fat in the first place. I only wish the why of it was anything like that simple, because understanding the whys of fatness is crucial to getting past the cycle of self-blame and chagrin that makes it so difficult for fat people to manage their weight and, even more important, prevents them from accepting who they are.

I have spent an awful lot of time trying to better understand my situation—reading, talking at length with doctors and nutritionists, pursuing my own therapy. Throughout this story I'll be grappling with the question of *why*. For now I'd just like to mention a few of the ideas we'll be exploring.

First, if there's one thing I've learned for sure, it's that being substantially overweight is a tremendously complex problem—and, therefore, the easy answers and simple formulas that are often dangled in front of us are seldom worth a damn.

Fatness involves chemistry as well as psychology, genetics as well as culture. Moreover, these several factors interact in varying ways in different individuals. No two people have the same genetic makeup or exactly the same metabolism. No two people have had the same array of childhood experiences.

On top of that complexity, there's the fact that what we *think* we know about fatness keeps changing. Nearly every week, it seems, there is some new "discovery" or revision to the accepted wisdom. A hormone is found that purportedly tells the body when it is full. A new study calls into question the health benefits of weight loss. Scientists argue; new data contradict previous assumptions. . . .

All this can be bewildering, even overwhelming. But at least it explains why simple answers about fatness generally lead on to more, and harder, questions.

So, then, why did I get fat? Let's start with the simplest and most obvious cause: I got fat because I ate too much. I took in more calories than I burned.

Can't get much simpler than that. But even here there is room for confusion—and, in some cases, denial—to creep in. Haven't we all known fat people who say they *don't* eat too much? Who claim they eat only normal portions, don't sneak food, and never binge? But even for people who are not chronic overeaters, there remains the question of what constitutes too much food for *them*.

There is no such thing as the "right" number of calories for everyone. It's completely individual, and it is one of life's ironies that fat people actually tend to burn fewer calories than lean people do. Muscle metabolism is faster than fat metabolism. In other words, the more fat you have, the less food it takes to put on more. No one said that life was fair.

Then there's the so-called famine response. Our bodies, unfortunately, are not equipped to recognize the difference between being on a diet and being starved. When we substantially reduce our food intake, our bodies do whatever they can to preserve energy—and weight. Our heart rate slows; we often feel cold and lazy. Bottom line: we burn fewer calories when we take in fewer calories.

I got fat, then, because I ate too much for my particular metabolism, and my metabolism, in turn, was affected by my efforts to lose weight.

But the real complexity begins when we peel back the next layer of the question: *why* did I eat too much?

Why did I sneak food when adequate food was readily available? Why did I hoard? Why did food, for me, become a focus of both passion and shame? Now we're approaching a mysterious and fertile realm where the diet gurus seldom go—and where some of the most important answers are to be found.

Nothing could be clearer to me than the fact that fatness is a matter of the mind as well as of the body, but the psychological aspects are poorly understood and seldom treated. Of the hundreds of "weight management" programs available, only a handful—generally very expensive, institution-based programs—even attempt to deal with the psychological problems of fat people. Most experts, frankly, duck the issue because they know so little about it. They treat what they know how to treat: the *symptoms* of fatness, not its causes.

But unless the causes are addressed, the symptoms recur. And keep recurring.

Like millions of other fat people, I've lost weight—lots of weight—on virtually every diet I've ever tried. To put it another way, almost any diet works as long as you stick to it. But the weight has always come back, sometimes more than I'd taken off. This yo-yo pattern is all too common. Why?

Again, simple answers are apt to be misleading; probably a mix of factors applies. Heredity may *incline* a person toward fatness. Glandular deficiencies may *predispose* someone to put on weight. But there are also psychological factors to consider.

Whether or not we like to admit it, many of us are dependent not only on food but also on being fat. Consciously, we want to be thinner; unconsciously, for reasons that tend to be both distressing and profound, we *need* to be fat. Between these two conflicting aspects of ourselves, what's going on is nothing short of war. As in any war, there are victories and setbacks, triumphs and humiliations. There is drama and there is violence, in the form of the psychic turmoil and anguish that so many fat people endure.

I've lived through plenty of that turmoil, and I know that weight itself is only one part of what I've had to contend with; another part—far more subtle and at least as painful—is the array of feelings that go with the weight. Feeling like a bad person because I can't control my eating. Feeling like a failure because I've gained back pounds I'd taken off. Feeling weak, feeling helpless, feeling just plain awful.

But I've also learned there is a way out of those bad feelings. It starts with acknowledging what a complex and powerful adversary fatness actually is.

Look, I was basically a good kid. I respected my parents. I didn't lie. I didn't steal. Yet I disobeyed and I lied and I stole to support my desire for food. Clearly, I was in the grip of something strong enough to bend my entire personality, to warp my most fundamental morality. Call it a compulsion, call it an addiction. The words can be argued, but the reality cannot. I was wrestling with something far beyond the reach of "willpower," far outside the realm of problems that can be solved by common insight.

Though it would be years before I became resigned to this, and more years before I learned to manage it effectively, it seems clear that, from the very start, I was wrestling with a disease.

CHAPTER 2

12 HOT DOGS
AND A MOVIE

When I was 12 years old I weighed 140 pounds. I wore "husky" clothes, and while my parents were clearly getting concerned about my weight, they thought of me as chubby, not fat. Still, I was fat enough to have earned a very unflattering nickname at school. A so-called friend of mine had started calling me "barrel of fudge" or sometimes simply "barrel." I answered to the names. I played along and smiled, as though it didn't matter. What else could I do?

As I and other boys my age reached puberty, our bodies began to change in dramatic and bewildering ways. Some kids had extreme growth spurts, adding half a foot of height in a year. Some seemed to shed their baby fat almost overnight, quite suddenly becoming angular and strong.

I had a kind of growth spurt, too; unfortunately, though, mine was east-west rather than north-south.

By my 14th birthday I'd gained 30 pounds, with very little increase in height. By the time I turned 15 I'd put on 30 more. This brought me to the psychological threshold of 200—and it seemed that, once I'd crossed it, there'd be no going back. I was no longer just a husky kid; I was a fat person. I'd come to that pivotal moment when overweight adolescents start to either thin down or keep on growing toward obese adulthood, and I hadn't even paused at the crossroads. By the time I graduated high school, I weighed 235. In 6 years I'd gained just shy of a 100 pounds, and I'd barely grown taller at all.

Make no mistake—I ate prodigiously during those years. My childhood sneaking and hoarding continued, and I kept finding new ways to chase down extra food. By now my family had bought a large freezer that we kept in the basement. My mother baked big batches of cookies and cakes, most intended to be frozen for future use. I'd raid the freezer, pilfering symmetrically in the continuing hope that my thefts would go unnoticed, and I'd gorge on sweets that were just barely defrosted.

But high school brings the beginnings of mobility and freedom, and the main thing that enabled me to take my overeating to a new level was the greater availability of food outside the home. When I was 16 I got my driver's license. This meant, for one thing, that I walked even less than I had before. It also allowed my father to "hire" me during summers and school vacations to drive a delivery truck for his laundry and dry-cleaning business. Now, I wouldn't necessarily say that truck drivers know where to find the best food in a given town, but they certainly know where to find big portions at fair prices. I soon knew all the most popular spots for doughnuts, hot dogs, and icy quarts of root beer. I knew where the ham sandwiches were the thickest, the rye bread the tangiest, the potato salad the richest. I ate up most of my wages as I snacked my way around Duluth.

As my weight grew more extreme and my fatness became the central fact of my public persona, I sometimes found myself engaging in behavior that was not exactly dignified; I played "the jolly fat man." I guess I figured that since everyone regarded me as the fat boy anyway, I may as well act the part.

I had a friend named Stu who was very tall and very 6 foot 5 and weighing about 325. He was the center on the football team, good enough at the sport to have had a serious flirtation with the idea of turning pro. Stu didn't move very well; then again, it was really hard for other people to move *him*. He and I had a party game we sometimes played. We'd take turns carrying each other across the room; at the end of each journey we had to drink a beer. The competition continued until one of us sagged under the load and could not complete the circuit. Stu usually won. He was bigger and stronger than I was, though the crucial difference was that he had a far greater capacity for beer.

Stu, like me, also had a vast capacity for food, and this earned us some very forced and uneasy smiles from the proprietors of the smorgasbord restaurants we sometimes visited. We cut a wide swath through a buffet; platters of herring, mountains of cold cuts, clustered helpings of desserts—all were laid waste by our youthful appetites, and there was more than a little bravado and competition in demonstrating how much we could eat.

If I enjoyed eating with Stu because we were so similar, I had another friend whom I liked to impress with my appetite because we were so different. He was a skinny, intense kid who played guitar and piano and could do a terrific Little Richard imitation. His name was Bob Zimmerman. We'd sometimes go to movies together, and there happened to be a hot-dog stand next to the theater.

They advertised "Coney Island" hot dogs topped with a delicious chili sauce. One evening Bob ordered a hot dog to take into the movies. I ordered a dozen. Bob seemed fascinated as he watched me munch them, one by one. (Bob later moved to Greenwich Village and changed his last name to Dylan. And he's still skinny!)

If I had some interesting friends in high school, I absolutely did not have a "regular" or fully satisfying social life. Specifically, I was almost entirely left out of the dating scene. Girls did not want to go out with the fat boy—it was that simple. They were nice enough to me during the school day and seemed to enjoy my conversation. But after dark, no way.

Was their aversion merely physical? Or did it also have to do with concerns about their own social status? Cool girls went out with cool guys: football players, track stars. Who, in that kind of environment, wanted to be known as the girlfriend of the fat guy? As I became more painfully aware of the girls' attitudes, I became ever more hesitant even to *try* to get a date. A bad cycle was starting up: since I didn't date, I missed out on opportunities to develop the specific social skills that went with dating. This eroded my confidence still further.

In any case, I spent a lot of Saturday nights alone. And

my loneliness gave rise to a dynamic that I'm sure will be familiar to many other people. Isolated by my fatness, I sought solace in food and grew still fatter. Feeling like an outcast, feeling awfully sorry for myself, I plunged headlong into the behavior that had made me "different" in the first place and took myself ever further toward the social fringe. Thus, with a strange economy, I could both comfort and punish myself with the very same activity: eating. Not infrequently, while my slimmer schoolmates were coupled up at the movies or necking in someone's car, I sat alone at the pizza parlor, wolfing down two whole pizzas and drinking a quart of Coke.

Now, I am well aware that some of the above details aren't pretty, and that some people will be uncomfortable with my reports of rampant and destructive overeating. But I am trying to keep the promise I have made myself: to accept responsibility while at the same time striving to shed guilt and leave shame behind. I don't think I am shirking if I say I don't believe that—at that stage of my life, at least—I could have behaved any differently than as I did.

Again, there is a paradox at work here. At each particular moment and with every bite of food I took in, I had a choice; by overeating so egregiously, I made the wrong choice again and again. But in some broader, deeper way, I don't believe I had a choice at all. Something was controlling me. What was it?

If the exact nature of the fat disease was still beyond my understanding, some of its implications were becoming painfully clear to me during those difficult years of adolescence. Being shunned for dates, hearing unkind nicknames, I was coming to know firsthand about our culture's deep biases against fat people.

Like every form of prejudice, those biases interfere with our being seen as individuals. Once someone got to know me, I became a person; I was Mike. But until that point was reached—if it ever was—I was just a stereotype, a silhouette, a cutout with a rounded shape not deemed to be attractive.

If the bias against fat begins as a prejudice regarding how we *look*, it ends up running much deeper. People tend to make all sorts of assumptions about those of us who are fat. They tend to think we're lazy. Sloppy. Clumsy. Weak. They tend to imagine that in some perverse way we have *chosen* to be fat and that we could be thin if only we'd get a grip and show some discipline, if only we'd rise up off our fat behinds and get some exercise. As if it were so easy! Unfat people tend to blame us for our burden—even though it's *our* burden, not theirs.

Not only do many people disapprove of us for being fat; they feel perfectly free to show it. Even now, in the 21st century, as we are finally becoming respectful of diversity in things like race and gender and sexual orientation, we as a culture still seem to condone sneering and smirking at fat people. Unfat people seem to think it's fine to stare at what we order in restaurants and to glare if it doesn't meet with their approval. Fat jokes are still a staple of so-called comedy on TV and in the movies. Fat stereotypes still abound. A fat man is likely to be presented as either falsely jolly or pathetic. A greedy politician will nearly always have an ample belly. A hero's sidekick may be portrayed as fat, for comic relief; the hero will, of course, be lean.

These insensitive representations of fat people are bad enough if we think of fatness simply as a human *difference*; they become completely inexcusable as we accept the idea that serious fatness isn't just a difference but a disease. Can you imagine civilized people making jokes about any other disease the way they make jokes about fat?

Now, whole books could be written about these sorts of cultural prejudices, but I just want to talk a little bit about them—not as theory or abstraction but because, in concrete ways, every day of our lives, those attitudes affect how fat people feel about themselves and their place in the world.

The first thing I want to point out is that, in most places, for most of history, people *wanted* to be fat. They *wished* they could be fat. For most of human history, most people haven't consistently had enough to eat. In the Old Testament, Pharaoh dreamed of seven fat calves and seven lean calves; Joseph understood this to mean that there would be seven years of good crops followed by seven years of famine. Fat, then, meant that times were good. Being fat was a sign of health and vigor and prosperity.

This attitude pertained to many different cultures. Look at old Chinese or Indian paintings: the powerful and wise are nearly always portrayed as fat. Why is Buddha pictured as having an enormous belly? His fatness is a symbol of his gravitas and serenity. In precolonial Africa, the great chiefs were fat, and their wives were even fatter; a man's prestige was measured by his ability to support a bevy of large women.

In Polynesia, being able to put on weight and keep it on was regarded as a positive because it offered the most practical of advantages. Polynesians colonized the Pacific by way of heroically long ocean voyages, in the course of which people had to live on near-starvation rations for weeks or months at a time. Those who began the journeys with ample reserves of body fat had a much better chance of surviving. Natural selection, then, *favored* fatness in the case of Polynesians; to this day, that group has a high incidence of obesity with no prejudice against it.

In Western culture, too, fatness was—until relatively recently—regarded as a good thing. Shakespeare's famous lines from *Julius Caesar* pretty well sum up the attitude. "Let me have about me men who are fat," Caesar says. In his view, fat men were reasonable, trustworthy, and nonviolent; they knew when they had it good. Cassius, by contrast, had "a lean and hungry look." He was grasping, furtive, and ruthless.

In Dutch paintings of the 17th century, leading citizens are generally plump, to say the least; the "prosperous paunch" was as an object of respect. Rubens's famously zaftig women put forth an ideal of feminine beauty that featured well-rounded bellies and formidable thighs. In 19th-century America, successful businessmen were expected to be beefy, as evidence of their wealth and rank. Even well into the 20th century, fat presidents like Taft and

Hoover kept alive the tradition of the "chief" whose size was a source of pride and reassurance for his subjects.

Now, I am not trying to stand the stereotypes on their heads or to argue that thin is bad and fat is good; a bias in *either* direction is wrong. What I am saying is this: attitudes about fatness are a form of fashion. They change; they go in and out of style. There is nothing *absolute* dictating that angular is attractive and round is not. How would Twiggy have been looked at in the age of Rubens? How would our svelte politicians have been regarded in the time of Caesar? Beauty may be in the eye of the beholder—but that eye, in turn, is conditioned by fads and fashions. Those of us who are fat are not *fundamentally* unattractive; we just have the bad luck of being out of sync with the currently accepted style.

That said, social fashion is very powerful, and however arbitrary the body-type preference at a given time, the prejudice is real enough. How virulent is today's bias against fat? I recently came across a study in which a group of college students were asked whom they would least like to marry. When the results were tallied, it turned out these students would rather be wed to a cocaine user, a former mental patient, a shoplifter, a sexually promiscuous partner, a communist, an atheist, or a blind person than someone who was fat. No wonder I had a tough time getting dates in high school!

Socially as well as physically, then, being fat makes life harder. That's a given; no use whining about it. Better to regard the added difficulty as a challenge and an opportunity—a chance to develop an extra measure of resourcefulness.

As a fat adolescent, I was forced to realize that the easy paths to popularity—athletic prowess, conventional good looks—were closed to me. I had to discover other ways to make myself appreciated. I noticed that many people really liked to talk; I taught myself to listen. I understood that some people flourished in the limelight; I learned how to be helpful behind the scenes. Along the way, almost without noticing, I was beginning to develop the skills and strategies that would enable me to grow into a reasonably successful and contented adult.

CHAPTER 3

LIGHT ON MY FEET

Around the Berman home when I was growing up, if we weren't eating, then chances were someone was singing.

My parents were both very musical; they'd met, in fact, while members of a synagogue choir. My mother and father both played the piano; I tried to get on good terms with that instrument but soon discovered it was not for me. Singing, on the other hand, came almost as naturally as breathing. I studied voice for a while and loved it. I'm not saying I was Mario Lanza, but I could belt out a show tune with great conviction.

Not only could my parents sing, they could dance. They made a terrific ballroom couple, and there were many evenings when we would go down to our basement rec room, play record after record, and my parents would twirl and glide across the floor. They taught me to dance, too. And, whether they realized it or not, this was one of the greatest gifts they could possibly have given to their fat, unathletic, and socially rather backward son.

Ballroom dancing—it might seem like a trivial, inconsequential thing, but to me it has been terrifically important. It was the first physical activity I felt confident about; the first thing my rotund body was *good* at. Dancing, my weight just didn't seem to matter. I was heavy on the scale, but somehow I was light on my feet. Doing the cha-cha or the rumba, I forgot about my size and melted into the movement. I felt graceful in a fox-trot, saw myself as elegant when I waltzed. When I threw myself into an energetic jitterbug, my usual sluggishness fell away, and I was vigorous and joyful.

As I've argued—and will argue again!—being fat makes many things more difficult . . . but it is no excuse for holding back from life. Dancing is one of the things that taught me this lesson.

I was, remember, the kid who was always picked last for sports teams. Slow and awkward, I had to be the catcher in baseball, the goalie in hockey. Those positions were not only unglamorous, they were dangerous. One day I got hit in the mouth with a bat. One time I was knocked unconscious by a hockey puck that nailed me square in the chin. I had some pretty good reasons to be leery of sports.

At the same time, in spite of my weight and my tendency toward solitude, I felt an urge to be active. Human bodies were made to *move*—and that includes fat human bodies too.

I'm not talking now about exercising to be virtuous; I'm talking about a fundamental need to use our muscles, get our blood flowing, revel in the animal vigor that's part of every one of us. So a kind of tug-of-war was going on inside me. Since sports had generally been humiliating, since running and even walking were an effort, I inclined toward physical laziness. At the same time, I ached for some exertion. I dimly understood what every couch potato knows down deep: sitting on the sofa might be easy, but it's also sort of depressing. It cheats us out of much of what is wonderful in life.

If the dilemma was a real one, the solution turned out to be quite simple. I just had to find something I was good at. It didn't have to be something that would earn me a varsity letter or make me a hero in team sports. It just had to be *mine*—something that suited my body and my skills, something that gave me pleasure and confidence.

That's what dancing did for me. I don't think it's over-stating to say that dancing is one of the things that started me on the way toward becoming my own person. I measured myself against no one when I danced. I shed my usual self-consciousness. On the dance floor, I was no longer Mike the Fat Guy; I was Mike the Pretty Smooth Dancer.

Dancing gave me not only a much-needed physical outlet but also a comfortable way to have contact with girls. Maybe I wasn't in demand on the dating front, but at dances, where one didn't need to show up with an escort, I never lacked for partners. I knew how to lead and could be counted on to get the steps right. Equally important, my father had made a point of teaching me good manners and imbuing me with a deep respect for women. I prided myself on being a gentleman, and I think girls liked and trusted me for that. Did this make up for not having a "real" girlfriend? No. But it was a lot better than spending Saturday night with an oily pizza box and a six-pack of Coke.

In other ways, as well, I began to put together a social life that worked for *me*. I threw myself with a passion into extracurricular activities.

Like many other youths for whom reality wasn't all

that rosy, I was attracted to the land of make-believe—the theater. At age 13 I made my debut in a little-remembered play called *Mother Is a Freshman*. I still recall one aspect of that performance: the script called for me to give one of the girls a quick peck on the cheek. It was the first time in my life I had ever kissed a female to whom I was not related by blood.

Given my musical background, I loved to perform in operettas. I usually ended up in character roles where my fatness was actually an asset, lending a big presence to the parts I played. *Finian's Rainbow. Of Thee I Sing. Carousel.* I performed in all those wonderful shows. As with my dancing, singing and acting provided me with the enormous pleasure and relief of disappearing for a little while, of taking a break from being me. When I performed, I entered a realm where I wasn't measured by my girth but by whatever modest skill and talent I possessed.

Since part of me still yearned to be one of the guys, I also found a way to keep some involvement with school sports. I became the student manager of the cross-country running team. I was the guy who carried the clipboard, fetched the towels, helped the coach remember where he'd put the stopwatch. The irony, of course, was that the cross-country runners tended to be the leanest, lankiest kids of all. But they were nice guys, and I enjoyed their company. Sometimes, during wind sprints, I'd join in the races. The distance was 100 yards, and I got a 40-yard head start. I generally finished last yet was not embarrassed. The other kids were good-natured and supportive, and that made all the difference.

If my physical energies were circumscribed by my weight, my mental energies seemed unaffected. I was curious about everything. I found that I had a certain knack for rhetoric. This led me to the speech team, where my size, I believe, was actually to my advantage; issuing forth from my big body, my words took on an extra authority. I also wrote for the school newspaper. And I discovered what has been the love of my working life: politics.

I managed my first political campaign at the tender age of 14, working on behalf of a girl who was running for president of our junior high student council. Why did I manage her campaign rather than run on my own? While I don't recall making a conscious decision, it now seems clear that my preference had to do with my fatness. Self-conscious about my weight, I was more comfortable staying in the background. Intuition told me that candidates had to be attractive, whereas managers only had to be hard-working, focused, disciplined, shrewd, determined, and resourceful. Since I realized that I wasn't cute, I understood that I had better work my tail off trying to become those other things.

When I was a teenager, then, I knew what it was like to feel different. I experienced the isolation and loneliness that went with the turf. I have no problem admitting that my welter of extracurricular activities was a way of compensating for that loneliness. At the time, I would have much preferred to be popular in the conventional way; it would have been so much easier if I was a football star, if my body was lean and my clothes fit stylishly. But that's not the hand I was dealt.

Over time, though—and largely without my noticing from day to day—I realized that something sort of wonderful had been happening. My various "compensations" had been adding up to a pretty good approximation of the sort of life I feared I'd never have. I was busy; I had friends; I was appreciated and respected for things I was good at.

And I had one further satisfaction that my effortlessly popular schoolmates would never know: I'd *earned* my social life. I'd worked at making it happen. It probably would have happened more readily if I'd been thin, but I doubt I would have learned as much.

Gradually, like most adolescents, I was learning how to take control of my life. Unfortunately, though, this developing sense of being master of my destiny did not extend to my weight. All through high school and into my college years, my weight just kept increasing.

By this time it was all too clear that my fatness wasn't just a "phase," nor was it merely a cosmetic issue. It was a chronic problem with real and potentially serious implications.

When I was 15, my father started me on a life-insurance program. He seemed to understand that my fatness might lead to early health problems. He also knew for a fact that my burgeoning weight would bring on steeply rising premiums and that there might even come a point when I couldn't get insurance at all.

This was scary stuff, and so my mother started taking me to an internist; this was before the phenomenon of diet doctors had taken hold, at least in our part of the world. My visits to the doctor were very instructive— mainly because nearly everything he said or did turned out to be wrong. He ascribed my fatness to a glandular problem I probably did not have. He prescribed a pill I probably did not need. He suggested an appetite suppressant that definitely did not work.

But before we get too smug about how primitive medicine was in 1955 and how wonderfully far we've come since then, let's keep a couple of things in mind. The doctor I went to was not a quack; he was, overall, a well-trained and careful physician who kept himself informed about the leading theories of the day. Those theories, in turn, were shiny and new, regarded as great advances over the ignorance that had reigned before.

My point is that new theories—and the products and services they give rise to—are *always* trumpeted as breakthroughs. Not to be cynical, but calling something a breakthrough is a time-honored way of getting someone to buy it. Why should we believe that today's "knowledge" is any more definite or final than that of 1955? Check back in a generation, and our own scientific "breakthroughs" might seem as naïve, quaint, or wrongheaded as those of the 1950s. This, in my view, is an excellent reason to be skeptical of silver bullets and miracle cures that tout themselves as "the latest," "the newest," "based on cutting-edge research," and so forth.

In any case, back in 1955, I was diagnosed as being hypothyroid. That was the standard diagnosis in those years. If you were fat, that meant you had a slow metabolism; since the thyroid gland—by way of its main hormone, thyroxine—controlled metabolism, that must mean your thyroid was deficient. The solution was to pop a pill with synthetic thyroxine in it.

Again, this was probably all wrong. First, I was probably not thyroid deficient, as later tests confirmed. But even if I had been, the treatment was unlikely to have been effective. Metabolism is way more complicated than was understood at the time: many things affect it; no single hormone controls it. As for those ubiquitous thyroid pills, it is now generally believed that taking such medications orally is no guarantee that they will function as hormones do when secreted naturally by the body, at a certain site and at certain times.

Oh, then there was the supposed appetite suppressant that came in the form of wafers. Unfortunately, I found them quite delicious and wolfed them down just like any other cookie. Frankly, I suspect they *were* like any other cookie. If they suppressed my appetite any more effectively than eating, say, half a stack of Oreos, I really didn't notice. I ate them and got hungry again.

My first foray into systematic weight loss, then, has to be chalked up as a failure. Even so, the experience constituted a certain rite of passage. Still in my midteens—and before the age of big-time, big-name, much-hyped diets had even started—I'd entered the world of conscious, chronic dieters. I'd stepped onto the merry-go-round. I'd become a charter subscriber to the commercial weight-loss sweepstakes.

Prior to this, I'd made some sporadic attempts to take off weight, efforts mostly prompted by my mother and consisting mainly of vague and soon-forgotten commitments to eat less. This was different; this was serious. This was the beginning of a lifelong quest, an unrelenting and at times desperate search. Eventually I would come to understand that I'd been searching in a lot of the wrong places, looking outside when the answers were within.

But in the meantime, I dieted. Dieting—which has become a rather sloppy shorthand for almost any attempt at losing weight—is an endlessly recurring theme in the lives of most fat people. My own adventures and misadventures with diets will be an unavoidably recurring feature of this story. For now, though, I'd just like to mention a single detail about the topic—a detail that, in my view, helps to explain why dieting is so difficult and so painful, and why diets, in the long run, seldom work. It has to do with the origin of the word itself.

Our word *diet* derives from the Greek *diaita*, which means, simply, "way of life." The same root gives rise to our words *day* and *daily*. In its original meaning, then, *diet* did not imply starvation, frustration, anxiety, dread, misery, hunger pangs, or guilt; it referred simply to how one lived from day to day—what one did, what one ate.

In its modern sense, *diet* means just the opposite; a diet is exactly what we *don't* do in the regular course of our lives. For those of us who eat with gusto, for whom food is not only nourishment but comfort, dieting is a harsh disruption, a rude denial. Dieting is at war with our *di-aita*—which is why being "on a diet" feels stressful and false and, above all, temporary.

For a diet to really work—for it to lead to long-term, sustainable weight loss, rather than just an episode of shedding pounds—it must become a way of life. Don't panic—this does not require permanent starvation or extreme self-denial. It *does* require the will and the focus to work through to a balanced regimen of eating and exercise, a strategy that aims at our overall well-being while taking honestly into account the extra difficulty that our fatness imposes.

This is what I mean by management.

CHAPTER 4

ME, A CHEERLEADER?

In case there's anyone out there who still believes that life is fair, consider this: by the time I started college, I was already beginning to go bald. Now, reasonable minds may differ as to how much responsibility I bear for being fat, but I categorically refuse to accept even a shred of blame for the fact that my hair was falling out. It came out in my hairbrush, in the shower drain, in the towel I used to dry myself.

The funny part is that I didn't much mind that I was going bald. It made me look older—and kids *want* to look older. As was the case with my weight, however, my mother actually seemed more concerned about my balding than I was. She insisted that we go to see a hair-loss expert.

The "expert" in this case was the ancient barber who had cut my father's hair for decades and now cut mine as well. Did he happen to know of a treatment for premature baldness? As a matter of fact, he did. The treatment consisted of making a fine paste from olive oil and cigar ash and rubbing it on my head several times a day. As it turned out, this remedy did not succeed in growing hair, but I do recall the aroma of that particular brand of olive oil even now.

Not one to give up easily, my mother sought a second opinion. This time we consulted with an elderly dermatologist. He told us he knew of only one thing that would stop my hair from falling: the floor. At that point my mother finally became resigned, and so did I. I was going bald; so be it.

I started college, then, weighing 235 pounds, with a rapidly receding hairline. This was not exactly a formula for campus popularity, but I was determined not to let it hold me back. I'd learned from my high school experience that part of having a social life was *deciding* to have a social life. Also, although it would be decades before I would formulate this in words, I think I was starting to live out the central tenet of my personal philosophy: that while it would certainly be nice to be thinner, the main idea was to learn how to be happy and successful.

I attended the University of Minnesota at Duluth—a

school of 1,900 students—and, though I continued to live at home, I threw myself with gusto into campus life. I competed on the debating team. I joined the Young Republicans Club. (*That* membership didn't last long!) I dodged the phys ed requirement by registering for a dance class; once again, ballroom dancing helped me to establish a social identity I felt okay about. I kept alive my tenuous connection to the world of athletics by becoming sports editor of the college newspaper. I continued in the theater, playing the character of Nicely, Nicely Johnson in *Guys and Dolls*. Clearly, this was a role a fat man could perform; Stubby Kay had played the part on Broadway.

False modesty aside, I must have been acquiring something of a reputation as a doer, because during the summer between my freshman and sophomore years I received a totally unexpected phone call from the university provost. This led to one of the stranger activities of my college years.

At the time, our school did not have its own football stadium; we played our home games at a high school field some miles away. The provost dreamed of building a new arena. The funds for the project would have to come from the members of Duluth's business community; that community, however, was concerned that there was not enough school spirit. Why donate to a college if even the students themselves didn't seem excited about the place? So the provost's request to me was simple: would I take on the job of building up school spirit? I asked some questions and accepted.

I decided that my first task should be to recruit a great new group of cheerleaders.

But who should be included in the squad? I decided to go not for previous experience but popularity. If the idea was to build esprit, then it seemed important to draw people in from all subsets of the student body—the jocks, the intellectuals, the fraternity and sorority set, and so forth. So I recruited young women who were stars in each of those groups. We had one experienced cheerleader who took charge of training the others. The squad then set about inventing new cheers and choreographing new formations.

Now, this hints at one of the great paradoxes of my college years. As a freshman, I hadn't had a single date. Not one. And here I was, surrounded by some of the school's most attractive and popular young women. We were pals; we had a lot of laughs together; yet I was keenly aware that I did not figure in any of their romantic plans.

There's no denying that my fatness disqualified me as boyfriend material. Being fat made me "safe" as a buddy and all but unthinkable as a lover.

I can't say I was thrilled about this, but at least I made the most of being a pal. I developed and savored my capacity for having close and honest friendships with women; this remains a cherished and rewarding aspect of my life.

But back to the cheerleading. *I* was part of the squad as well, and once we'd choreographed the leaps and pom-pom routines for the women, that left the question of what I would do.

I weighed more than 250 pounds by then; I wasn't about to turn cartwheels or propel myself skyward off a trampoline. So I devised a different sort of grand entrance for myself. At the first football game under the new regime, I led the cheerleaders in a procession around the track that circled the field. While they jogged, I pedaled a miniature girl's bike. I wore a cheerleading sweater, shorts, and kneesocks; I also sported a freshman beanie and a raccoon coat. Strapped to my back was a power megaphone through which I led the cheers.

This crazy spectacle made such a hit that we reprised it for hockey season—with the difference that the women came in on ice skates! When it was time for basketball, we adapted the procession to fit within the confines of the gym. School spirit did in fact take off; several years later, the provost got his stadium.

I smile as I recall this episode—it *was* pretty funny, after all—but I smile with an intense ambivalence. In my kneesocks and beanie and raccoon coat, I know I looked ridiculous. Anyone would have looked ridiculous in that getup; that was the whole idea. In point of fact, though, it wasn't *anyone* parading around like that; it was me. What qualified me for the role, and added to the comedy, was my fatness. In a very public way, I was once again doing the "jolly fat man" routine. And I can't say I feel very proud of those instances when I compromised my dignity for a laugh or stooped to fulfilling a stereotype.

At the same time, in leading the cheerleaders I was doing something *good*. I was keeping my commitment to the provost and benefiting my school. To accomplish that, I used what I had—my organizing skills and also my size. I sometimes wonder if perhaps we get so hung up on the question of our *external* dignity—the dignity of our appearance—that we think too little about the deeper dignity that has to do with an honest sense of who we are and what we have to give.

Besides, are fat people supposed to hide? Physical size, after all, is a pretty obvious characteristic. Are we supposed to pretend our differences do not exist? Should we spend our whole lives skulking around in modest black or purportedly slimming vertical stripes and kid ourselves that unfat people will see us as being just like them?

I have no answers for questions like these; they reflect ambivalences I've lived with for many years. I can't resolve them; I can only report on them. But I believe they are worth pondering. They are part of the reality that fat people deal with every day.

During my first two years of college, at a stage of life when my growth in height was already finished, I put on another 33 pounds. By the end of sophomore year, I weighed 258.

Looking back, I really don't know why this happened. It seems to me that it shouldn't have. I had a full and busy life. I was reasonably active and basically happy. Still, the pounds kept accumulating. When I try to come up with an explanation, two images come to mind. In different ways, each image says something significant—and cautioning—about our society's approach to food.

The first image is of Bridgeman's Ice Cream Parlor. A

Duluth landmark in those years, Bridgeman's featured rich and creamy ice cream. I don't think anyone had heard of "low fat" at the time. "Sugar free" existed, as I recall, but it was dreadful stuff, reserved for diabetics. As for frozen yogurt, that wasn't yet even a glimmer in a food marketer's eye. What Bridgeman's served was the full-throttle, megacaloric product.

But the point I'd like to make is not about how good or even how rich that ice-cream was; it's about how *much* of it they served. Whatever the quality, the clear emphasis was on quantity.

Bridgeman's signature offering was a sundae called the Lollapalooza. It consisted of many scoops of ice cream, clustered together like boulders at the bottom of a rock-slide. Each scoop had a different topping—hot fudge, caramel, chopped walnuts in heavy syrup—and the whole thing was topped by a mountain of whipped cream. That sundae was vast. It was so big that two people often shared one.

As part of its promotional efforts, Bridgeman's had put forth a standing offer: Anyone who could eat a whole Lollapalooza would receive a certificate commemorating the feat. Anyone who could finish *two* Lollapaloozas at a sitting would get both desserts for free.

It probably won't surprise you that I earned one of those certificates, which hung for many years in my old room at my parents' house—or that on at least one occasion I polished off two giant sundaes, on the house.

Now, you can't blame ice-cream merchants for wanting to sell ice cream, any more than you can blame McDonald's for wanting to sell burgers or Krispy Kreme for hawking doughnuts. Selling food is what they do; deciding what to eat is what *we* do. As I've argued, eating is a matter of personal responsibility, and it's no one's fault but my own that I elected to eat two Lollapaloozas at a sitting.

That said, the choices we make are conditioned by many factors. For those of us who have the fat disease, our personal chemistry and compulsions cannot be overlooked. But there are cultural issues as well. We all like to believe that we are "free"; and, strictly speaking, we are. But it is naïve and counterproductive to ignore the ways in which our freedom is tempered by societal influences and pressures.

Our culture glorifies excess, and not only in matters of food and eating. Think about the crazy tail fins on 1950s cars. Think about multi-million-dollar halftime shows at football games. Think about Las Vegas. American society operates on the premise that bigger is better. We are the land of supersize French fries, six-foot submarine sandwiches, and all-you-can-eat restaurants—where the food is barely acceptable and the only reason to go is that there's a lot of it.

Again, if I were a disciplined, "healthy" eater, I could move through this supersize landscape unscathed. I would not have eaten two Lollapaloozas. I would not have eaten *one* Lollapalooza. I would have had a scoop of ice cream and been content.

But I'm not a healthy eater. I am, I believe, an eater with an addiction. That's my problem, not society's. But our culture enables my addiction and legitimizes my compulsion by fostering the belief that overeating is not just good for the local economy, but it's also good, clean fun. Why else send an overeater home with a certificate, as if he'd accomplished something heroic?

To put this in perspective, it's worthwhile to remember that other cultures have quite different attitudes about food. A recent *New York Times Magazine* article titled, fittingly enough, "Our National Eating Disorder," makes the point that various cultures—older cultures—have evolved unwritten, commonsense rules about eating. These "rules" encourage eating healthily because they are based on long and practical observation of what *works*.

Over time, these practical habits take on the force of tradition. Food traditions, in turn, free people from worrying about what's "healthy" to eat; people from those cultures eat reasonably because doing so has become a component of good manners, a way of showing respect for social custom.

For example, the French and Italians, who have endless supplies of sinful cheese and legendary desserts, are far less fat, as nations, than we are. Part of the reason, at least, is that those cultures don't encourage overeating by winking at it; they look down on it. Overeating is, for them, a violation of decorum, a show of disrespect to the food itself and the communal traditions of the table. Europeans look at overeating the way Americans might look at blowing cigarette smoke into someone else's face. It's just bad form.

In recent years, my business has taken me to Europe quite often, and I can testify that, by American standards, European entrées are modestly proportioned and European desserts are tiny: narrow little wedges of tarte tatin; squares of chocolate cake barely bigger than petits fours. Even the fabled cheese courses are not excessive; it's a taste of this, a nibble of that. The idea is to tantalize, not overwhelm. No Lollapaloozas for them! It's a matter of tradition, and if it ever got to be a tradition with us, we'd probably be better off.

Talking about the social component of eating leads me to the second image I recall from those early years of college. It's an image of the small basement kitchen where I prepared and ate so many meals alone.

As I've said, I lived at home even after starting college; but, to give myself more privacy, I moved to the lower level of the house. Privacy meant, in part, that I no longer had to sneak food or to hide my little stashes. I did my own shopping. I bought whatever I wanted, as much as I wanted. I prepared the food myself and got to be a pretty decent cook.

All of that was fine, of course—a normal part of growing up and becoming independent. But the case can be made that, for those of us who tend to be problem eaters, eating alone is really dangerous.

Consider, by analogy, the folklore about the difference between a "social" drinker and a "problem" drinker; the former tends to drink with other people, while the latter tends to drink alone. When you drink—or eat—alone, it's hard to know when you should stop. The usual standards seem not to apply when nobody is watching. For those of us who have trouble with the concept of "enough," solitude compounds the difficulty.

Traditional food cultures seem to have figured this out, and they discourage solitary dining. Families eat together; friends seek out friends. Dinners are leisurely affairs; people eat more slowly because time is made for conversation. Since we all know that the feeling of being full lags behind the act of eating, eating more slowly means you'll probably eat less. Moderation is further enforced by the simple good manners that go with sharing.

In Europe, even business travelers, those loneliest of people, are encouraged not to eat alone. If they lack for companions, they can usually find restaurants with communal tables, where strangers can enjoy a few hours' chitchat with their meal. American business travelers, it seems, are far more likely to pull on a bathrobe, call room service, and hunker down in front of the television. Who cares about restraint, table manners, or how much or how fast you eat, when you're all by yourself in the privacy of your room?

Again, I'm not saying that our culture makes people fat. Eating too much makes people fat. But our individual tendencies are confirmed and reinforced by social customs.

For myself, moderation has always been an elusive concept; our society, with its assumption that bigger is better, makes it all too easy for me to overdo it. Take, for example, one of my current favorite treats: Frappuccinos from Starbucks. They come in three sizes—Tall, Grande, and Venti—containing 190, 250, and 350 calories, respectively. I have never ordered a Tall and seldom ask for a Grande; the Venti is available, and I go for it.

Similarly, I have had, since childhood, a regrettable tendency to be furtive in matters of food, to perpetuate my overeating by hiding it; our cultural acceptance of eating alone reinforces my private problem.

Now, I can't change the food culture that is all around me. I can't tell the Cheesecake Factory to serve smaller slices or ask the fast-food chains to stop putting sugary soft drinks in cups the size of barrels. But I *can* be more aware of the traps and hazards that are strewn across the landscape. If we fat people are to take control of our weight and our lives, it's helpful to confront and try to understand the whole array of influences that act on us. Some of those influences are outside our own skins, our own metabolisms, our own psyches. Some of them are cultural—as American as an all-you-can-eat buffet.

CHAPTER 5

WHETHER TO LAUGH
OR CRY

When I was a sophomore in college, I was invited to join a fraternity.

The invitation, frankly, surprised me. I did not think of myself as typical fraternity material. Then again, the fraternity that rushed me wasn't typical either. It consisted mainly of slightly older guys, many of whom were Korean War veterans attending college on the GI Bill. They'd seen a great deal more of life than the typical undergraduate had, and their values were that much more developed. I like to think they were able to look past my fatness and see me as a solid person, potentially a good friend.

There were no frat houses on campus, but a number of our members had great apartments nearby, and our parties were considered some of the best. Suddenly I had a much easier time getting dates. As I couldn't help but realize, however, the girls I asked to these parties were more interested in the parties than in me. I was their ticket to get in the door. Once inside, they tended to drift off and mingle with my older, smoother, thinner buddies.

Over time, my romantic woes became a topic of conversation among a few of my fraternity brothers. As I've said, they were worldly guys—with all that connoted in 1959. I was not a worldly guy. To put it bluntly, I was still a virgin. For a college sophomore, this was not as unusual as it would become a decade or so later, when the sexual revolution was really up and running; still, there's no denying that I was lagging the curve, and my well-meaning frat brothers decided they should help.

Sometime later, there was a party at a lakeside cabin near Duluth. Discouraged by the outcome of some of my previous "dates," I decided to go stag. Quite to my surprise, an attractive woman a couple of years older than myself seemed to be paying attention to me. I knew her slightly. She was a regular at our parties, and she had always seemed to be attached to one or another of the older members. She'd always been nice to me . . . but nothing more.

Sometime around 10:30 or 11, I began to notice that some of my buddies seemed to be watching us, then exchanging little smiles, and gradually I caught on to the game. They had fixed things up for me. This woman had agreed to introduce me to sex as a favor to my friends. Maybe it wasn't an ideal scenario—no candlelight, no violins—but God knows it was better than nothing.

Sure enough, around midnight my companion took me by the hand, and we walked off toward one of the bedrooms. She entered first, moved toward the bed, kicked off her shoes, and lay down. She motioned for me to join her; her manner was hardly passionate but at least I believed it was *friendly*. . . . As I approached the bed, however, I saw that she had passed out cold.

I didn't know whether to laugh or cry. I was awfully disappointed but also strangely relieved. I covered her with a blanket, went back to the party, and later told my buddies that we would not repeat that experiment.

Whether to laugh or cry. This, of course, is a universal human dilemma. As some wise person once observed, life is a comedy to those who think and a tragedy to those who feel; and since human beings do both, a lot of our experience takes place on the cusp between laughter and tears. But I can't help thinking that fat people must face the question of whether to laugh or cry a bit more often than most. That's why the stereotype of the jolly fat man exists right alongside the patronizing notion that fat people are deserving of sympathy. Being fat seems to give rise to situations that can be viewed as either very sad or totally ridiculous.

Part of the reason for this is, I believe, simple geometry. Fat people literally do not fit so well in a world designed for unfat people. This gives rise to all kinds of clashes in size and shape, awkward situations that—depending on your point of view—are either deeply embarrassing or the stuff of slapstick comedy.

For me, among the minor indignities of college were those one-piece half-wraparound chair-desks that were part of so many classrooms. As my volume kept expanding, those chairs grew ever more uncomfortable. The desk part cinched my stomach. The thickness of my arms and chest made it difficult to write on the small surface provided. I felt extremely self-conscious sitting there, knowing I was overflowing the confines of the undersized seat, that there was an obvious disproportion between the furniture and its occupant.

I could, I suppose, have asked for some kind of special seating. But it didn't even occur to me to do that. Special seating, special *anything*, was exactly what I didn't want. It would only draw even more attention to my size and make it even clearer that I was different.

A few years later, when I was in law school, I had my ultimate misadventure with a piece of furniture. In the student lounge, where I spent a fair amount of time reading and socializing, there were wooden armchairs—the kind you see at clubs and such, with a crest on the top part of the back. For me, the chairs were somewhat snug but otherwise quite comfortable.

One day, I got up from my chair . . . or, rather, I *tried* to get up from my chair. Halfway out of the thing, it became clear that I was stuck. My body had essentially flowed out to fill the space between the arms and the seat. My hips were captured; my bottom stayed glued to the chair, and the whole thing lifted up with me as I tried to stand. For a horrified moment I was suspended there, crouched over, grappling with the furniture in a very public place. I felt all eyes on me, understood that people didn't want to look but, as at a train wreck, couldn't turn away.

Whether to laugh or cry? I decided in a heartbeat to play the situation as a comedy. Rather than go through painful contortions to free myself from the chair, I simply let it cling to me. Still crouched over, taking small, constricted steps, I carried it across the room, somewhat like a turtle with its shell, and sat down once again. Among those who had noticed my dilemma, there was an almost palpable sense of relief as people realized I was treating the episode as a joke. What I was feeling inside was another matter. But, faced with the unappealing choice of either playing the jolly fat man or being seen as an object of sympathy, I opted for the former.

Through the years of my adolescence and early manhood, I worked extremely hard at fitting in. Realizing that I would have to earn a social life, I threw myself into activities and situations. Understanding that popularity did not come easily to fat guys, I put forth extra effort to make myself of use. But however much progress I might make in this figurative form of fitting in, the literal sort remained a frustration and a problem.

Is it a coincidence that we use the same phrase to describe, on the one hand, being at ease with our peers and, on the other hand, being well matched to the furniture? Do we have to fit the chair in order to fit in with the group? Does social comfort imply a certain conformity of shape and size?

As a fat man, I certainly hope not. Sure, I'd like to be more comfortable in a standard chair, but I cannot accept the notion that my fitting in with people is dependent on my relationship with objects that clearly were not designed with me in mind.

 At the end of my senior year of college, I was given an award for leadership in campus affairs. This recognition meant more to me than any academic honors I might have earned. It confirmed that I had made a contribution. Beyond that, it suggested that I had gotten past at least some of the limitations imposed by my fatness. Maybe I wasn't doing such a great job of controlling my weight, but at least I was making real progress in the crusade not to let my weight control *me*.

When I think back over my last 2 years as an undergraduate, what strikes me is how public many of my activities were. I continued my exploits in the theater, playing the baron in *The Madwoman of Chaillot* and the father in *Summer and Smoke*. I got involved in other media as well. Starting with an unpaid internship in a local TV newsroom, I moved on to a part-time job as a news reporter at a radio station.

Radio is a perfect place for a person who's self-conscious about his appearance. Radio studios are wonderfully cozy and private; the voice goes out to people's living rooms while the face and body remain a secret. It's a little surprising, then, that in my senior year I went back to television, becoming a part-time reporter at the largest station in the local market. Being a very low-level employee, I generally did my own camera work and was behind the lens much more often than in front of it. At times, though, I did appear on-screen and had to confront a situation that many people, fat and otherwise, find painful: I had to shed defenses and illusions and see myself as others saw me—bulky and balding.

Given my self-consciousness about my size, why did I put myself in so many situations of exposure? Probably I was compensating—compensating for my fear of being lonely and left out; compensating for my tendency to hide. But I would argue that there's nothing wrong with compensating if it leads to good results. It is well known that many of our most successful businessmen tend to be short; their wealth and power compensate for their height. Other high achievers are compensating for a lack of mother-love or reacting against the slights of overcritical fathers. Every life has its challenges; those challenges define not only the hurdles that we face but also the victories that are possible. For me, a fat man, becoming reasonably comfortable in public situations was a victory.

In more private matters, too, the second half of my college years provided evidence of progress. Junior year I had my first real romance. The lady in question was a freshman and an English major. She was interested in creative writing; I was by that time the editor of the school paper. Suddenly it seemed clear that what the paper needed was more creative writing; a whole new section, in fact! My amour thus became a published author. I even persuaded our photographer to do a portrait of her that ran on the first page of the new feature; it was a very arty, very early-1960s image: the young writer sitting in a tree, looking soulful.

The romance didn't last long, a mere six weeks or so. Sexually, we never made it past the heavy-petting stage. Still, the relationship was sweet and genuine, and it did wonders for my confidence. I could finally believe that at least some women might be attracted to me, that my fatness did not altogether disqualify me as a love interest. After that first overdue relationship, I became a great deal more relaxed with women; being more relaxed, in turn, made it a much easier for other relationships and friendships to develop.

Somehow, I also lost more than 25 pounds during my last two years as an undergrad. I wish I could tell you how it happened, but I really don't know. This, I think, must be an aspect of the disease I have. In other compartments of my life, I'm pretty good at analyzing facts, synthesizing information, and figuring out the *why* of things. When it comes to my weight, even though I think and fret about it every day, real insight was, for many years, extremely difficult to come by; certainly it was at that stage of my life.

I could count calories and make lists of everything I ate, but this compiling of data and detail didn't quite add up to effective understanding. There simply seemed to be times when I was relatively disciplined about my eating and times when I was much less so. During my last two years of college, I was not following any particular regimen or sticking to any specific diet. I was trying to eat less and, for a while, I succeeded.

"For a while," unfortunately, is the key phrase here.

Three years later, when I was 25 and getting set to graduate from law school, I weighed just shy of 290 pounds. I'd put back everything I'd lost, plus another 20 or so.

Why? Again, it would be nice if I could come up with a tidy, logical, and persuasive answer.

Was it because law school was so stressful? No, I didn't find it especially stressful. I worked hard, but I was not a grind, and I kept my life in balance with my accustomed range of extracurricular activities.

Was it because I was unhappy? No, I don't recall that those years were an unhappy time. I had friends; I was actually pretty popular. I joined a law fraternity and was elected president. We had parties at the frat house, and I taught nurses how to dance. Life was pretty good.

Was it because I was homesick? No, I enjoyed being in Minneapolis. Besides, it was hard to be homesick when my mother kept sending care packages full of cookies and cakes, all my favorite things from her baking repertoire.

The bottom line, then, is the same old compulsive story. I gained weight because I ate too much. I ate too much because I could not control my appetite. I could not control my appetite because something was driving me—something that was beyond the reach of willpower, outside the realm of reason. From year to year I was slowly learning how to manage my disease, to recognize its quirks and patterns, and to live successfully in the face of it—but I don't kid myself that I was getting cured.

In my final year of law school, 1964, I started going to Weight Watchers, though I stuck with it for only a couple of months or so. Now that I think about it, this was somewhat analogous to my first real romance—less a serious, substantive relationship than a rite of passage, a gateway to a different stage of life. The age of brand-name, commercial diets was suddenly upon us, and I was right there with it, launching into my own career as a chronic sampler of many weight-loss programs.

Our Weight Watchers group met in a nearby suburb, and there was much that I liked about it. The overall approach seemed rational and sane. The regular weigh-ins gave people realistic short-term goals to aim at. The group leader seemed compassionate and bright, and the members seemed to be sincerely rooting for each other.

That said, there was something about the group that bothered me and was probably my main reason for leaving: there was almost nobody *like me*. There was almost no one who was young and almost no one who was male. Then as now, women seemed willing and able to talk openly about fatness as an issue in their lives, and men did not. The result was that I attended meetings meant to foster a sense of community and peer support but went away feeling every bit as isolated and different as I had before. Who knows—maybe this book began to germinate in the wake of those meetings, as I realized with frustration that fat men made things harder for themselves by holding in so many thoughts and feelings.

In any case, by the time I graduated law school and was ready to go out into the world, I was getting dangerously close to breaking through the 300-pound plateau. Paradoxically, though, my weight seemed to be less of an overwhelming factor in my life. I was a fat man, yes, but I wasn't *only* a fat man. I'd learned some things about myself, developed some other resources. I knew I had a capacity for hard work. My experience with student elections had confirmed my passion and instincts for politics. I'd learned to be a good listener and an effective persuader. Like everyone else who ever lived, I had my strengths and I had my weaknesses, my good points and my bad points. Flawed but undaunted, I was ready to be a grown-up.

Not that one ever leaves one's early years entirely behind. The habits and conflicts of childhood and adolescence tend to stay with us. Certainly this is true in matters of eating—especially problem eating.

I can still remember, from my law-school years, going back to Duluth for occasional weekend visits with my family. My mother would greet me at the door— standing back at first to behold me in all my volume, then coming forward to give me a hug. She would pinch my cheeks, and, with a mix of love and disapproval, affection and chagrin—a blend that only close family can muster—she'd say, "Oh, you are so fat!"

Then we'd sit down for a sumptuous dinner of brisket and potatoes, or roast chicken with a noodle pudding, followed by pie or layer cake or Toll House cookies—all the hugely fattening foods I'd savored as a child and that were equated in my mind with comfort and safety and warmth and love.

PART 2
ONE MAN, TWO LIVES

CHAPTER 6

LOVE IS BLIND,
SORT OF

In 1964, while studying for the bar exam, I signed up for my first real-world political campaign: the reelection effort of Lyndon Johnson. In anticipation of the possibility that Minnesota native and then senator Hubert H. Humphrey would be selected to complete the ticket, Minneapolis was already becoming one of the hubs of campaign activity. For a budding political junkie like myself, this was heaven, and I couldn't wait to get involved.

My first job, as an unpaid volunteer, was one of great import. For hours on end I sat in the basement of the Minneapolis city hall, hand copying information from voter registration cards. Remember, this was long before computers or even card sorters. JFK had only recently been assassinated. Vietnam was not yet a central issue. The

Beatles and other British rock groups were dominating the U.S. airwaves. It was a different world, and, at the age of 25, I found it full of opportunity and excitement.

Shortly after I took the bar exam, I received a promotion. I was actually put on the payroll! I was hired to lead the Johnson campaign's voter registration drive in a suburban congressional district. The pay was 50 bucks a week.

By a truly remarkable coincidence, the day I began that first paid job—August 1, 1964—was also the day I met the woman who would become my wife.

We met on a blind date. That in itself was improbable because, by that stage of my life, I had probably sworn off blind dates half a dozen times. My experience with blind dates had been excruciating. The details varied from disaster to disaster, but the general pattern was always the same. The women involved were put off by my fatness and couldn't help but show it. They seemed physically standoffish and gave the distinct impression that they were embarrassed to be seen in public as the escort of a fat man—as if being with a fat man cast doubt on their own attractiveness.

I was very sensitive to these slights; arguably I became *over*sensitive to them after I'd felt them a few times. In response, I tended to go to one of several extremes. Either

I'd get sulky and try to end the evening early, thereby fulfilling my assumption that *she* wanted to end the evening early, or I'd find myself trying way too hard to prove what a nice and fascinating guy I was, even though it was clear that there was no real interest on either side. Or I'd just avoid dating altogether—not a satisfying solution, but a safe one, and the final self-fulfilling prophecy on my chances for a love life.

Now that I think of it, I wonder why the women with whom I was lined up weren't better prepared to confront the reality of my weight. Hadn't the would-be matchmakers told them I was fat? Being well-meaning friends, maybe they'd been more tactful than accurate in their descriptions. Maybe they'd said I was "chubby" or "a little heavy" or simply "big." This is why I so dislike those well-intentioned euphemisms. They end up misleading people, and that's no help to anyone.

Alternatively, maybe my blind dates *had* been told that I was fat, and maybe they were unaware of the depth of their own biases and the strength of their gut reactions to a fat man until they saw me standing in the doorway. Either way, my past attempts at blind dating had accomplished nothing except to depress me, and I had no intention of putting myself in that situation again.

I suppose I agreed to that fateful date in 1964 because my sister, Sheila, asked me to do it as a favor to her. Sheila was then in her final year of college, studying speech pathology. In a clinical practicum at a local rehabilitation center, she had an instructor named Carol Podhoretz. Carol was new in town and knew almost no one. Sheila found her smart and interesting—and probably thought it would win her a few points to get the teacher a date. At first I resisted; my sister cajoled, and I finally agreed.

But I was dubious from the start, and my reservations intensified as I rang the doorbell to Carol's apartment and noticed that the door had a peephole. I suspected that I was being critically examined. Sure enough, Carol opened the door and greeted me with polite reserve, announcing that she had a terrible headache and would be unable to go out.

Frankly, her story didn't wash. She was clearly dressed for going out. Did she go to all the trouble of putting on stockings and makeup and a nice pair of shoes, *then* realize she wasn't feeling well? No. As Carol herself would later acknowledge, she was rejecting me because of my fatness. She was 24 years old; appearances were important to her, and mine was unacceptable.

But Carol was (and is) a naturally gracious person, and she suggested that I at least come in for a drink. I would just as soon have gone home and sulked, but I accepted. We started talking and found we had similar values. We were both intrigued with politics; I liked hearing about her interest in doing work that helped people. She later told me that she thought I was a really decent guy. After a horribly awkward start, we seemed to be quite comfortable in each other's company. An hour's conversation flew right by, then Carol announced that her headache was much better and she'd be happy to go out, if I still wanted to.

We had dinner at my favorite restaurant, then went to a club to dance. As I've mentioned, dancing was one of the few physical activities I felt confident about. Bodies change somehow when they're in motion; moving with the music, my body no longer seemed a liability. As for Carol, it turned out she was a terrific dancer; in fact, she'd been an instructor at an Arthur Murray studio. Gliding around the dance floor, we felt good about each other and good about ourselves. Somewhere between the cha-cha and the Lindy we began to have the feeling that it would be nice to see more of each other.

We went out on 29 of the next 30 nights. Then, in early

December, at a family dinner celebrating Sheila's college graduation, Carol proposed marriage, and I accepted. We made it official with a ring at Christmastime, which coincided with Carol's birthday, and set a wedding date of August 15 of the following year.

At the time of our engagement, I weighed 288 pounds—close to my heaviest to date. And I made one of the rashest promises I have ever made in my life. I told Carol I would be 50 pounds lighter by our wedding day.

Even now, I'm not sure why I made that promise. Clearly, part of my motivation was a desire to please Carol. She'd fallen in love with me *in spite of* my weight (or that's certainly how it seemed to me), but that didn't mean she was comfortable with it or that it wasn't an issue in her mind. So I think my promise was, in part, a kind of wedding gift to her.

But I also made that promise for myself. I'm not without periodic vanity; I wanted to look good on my wedding day. Also, with the 300-pound threshold looming not so far ahead, I knew I had to get a grip. Maybe I imagined the momentous change that was about to take place in my life could somehow pry me loose from the compulsions that had plagued me since childhood. Maybe, now that I'd found love, food would lose some of its power over me. Maybe, on the brink of marriage, I would become a slightly different person from the one I'd always been; maybe managing my weight would get easier.

It didn't happen; you can't shed a disease just by entering a different phase of life. My compulsions stayed with me. I struggled like crazy to lose those pounds.

Part of the difficulty was that I'd given myself too much time to do it. I had seven and a half months to lose a little less than 20 percent of my body weight. I now know that losing that percentage—and, more important, doing it in a way that is sustainable—constitutes a serious accomplishment. Back then I was somewhat cavalier about it. Twenty percent didn't strike me as a radical loss, and I felt no sense of urgency. I eased into the campaign, and there was plenty of backsliding early on.

One evening Carol and I were playing bridge with another couple. The hostess served coffee and chocolate cake. She handed me an extra-jumbo slice, as people often do. I don't know if this is well-intentioned but misguided generosity or simply an unconscious act; either way, it's really pretty irritating. The assumption seems to be: you're fat; ergo, you must want the biggest piece of cake. In this case, I reinforced the stereotype by wolfing down the dessert without a thought.

Later, in the car, it became clear that Carol was furious. I apologized and vowed to be more careful. I broke the vow almost at once.

It happened on a weekend when my mother was visiting. We went to a deli for breakfast, and I ordered one of my favorite dishes, an egg soufflé. Now, you'd be hard-pressed even to imagine a more caloric preparation. The soufflé was made from clarified butter, three eggs, cheddar cheese, Swiss cheese, and American cheese, all whipped together and baked in a ramekin, so no fat could possibly escape. Why did I order it? Was it just plain gluttony? Self-destructiveness? A moment of simple inattention? All I can say for sure is that it's what I felt like eating.

So I ordered it, and an extremely unpleasant little scene followed. Carol said something critical of my choice. Hurt and embarrassed, I got up and walked out in a snit. I later learned that my mother had felt compelled to stand up for her son and had words with Carol about how harsh she'd been to me.

The irony is that, if my mother and I had been break-fasting alone, *she* probably would have criticized my choice of the soufflé. I can remember at least one other incident when I shot myself in the foot regarding my promise to lose weight for the wedding. Again, the scene of the crime was a delicatessen; Carol sat across from me, shaking her head in disapproval or maybe disbelief. At the same meal, I ate a Reuben plus a heel of pickled cow's tongue. Aside from the massive intake of calories, I was flirting with a wicked case of heartburn! Again I raise the question, *why?* Again I have no satisfying answer. I knew I was making it harder to keep my promise. I knew I was making Carol angry as well as disappointing myself. I couldn't help it.

Eventually, faced with a shortening deadline, I got serious and somewhat desperate about taking off the weight. I used several different approaches, including a high-fat diet that was in fashion at the time. But I made no real changes in my lifestyle; which is to say, I did nothing to guarantee that this somewhat frenzied weight loss would be anything more than a fleeting episode. I added no regular exercise; I denied myself food but failed to alter the fundamentals of my relationship with food. Still, by our wedding day I had fulfilled my promise. I'd dropped 53 pounds and weighed a quite presentable 235.

A large picture from our wedding hangs in our apartment, and I see it every day. I must say I looked pretty good. Unfortunately, I must also say that seldom had anyone worked harder to fit into a tuxedo he would almost at once outgrow again.

Let's return now to the notion of the food cop.

As I've mentioned, it's my belief that many fat people have one or more food cops in their lives. Maybe it's a parent, or a spouse or lover, or a well-meaning close friend. Whatever the specifics of the relationship, the role of the food cop remains the same: to influence the eating habits of the fat person. The influence may be direct or indirect. Techniques employed range from gentle cajoling to relentless browbeating to simply hiding the cookies. Positive reinforcement—in the form of lavish praise for eating well—can be an effective though sometimes patronizing tool. Negative reinforcement—as in wilting criticism of the fat person's eating choices—tends to make for unpleasant mealtimes but certainly gets attention.

In the great majority of cases, the food cop is motivated by caring and concern. But that doesn't mean that his or her well-intentioned input is always kindly received. The food cop inserts him- or herself between the fat person and his or her cravings. Clearly, this is a formula for tension and conflict. For a compulsive eater like me, obstacles that stand in the way of my food desires are made to be trampled. I'm not likely to be gracious to someone who's trying to thwart my appetite, even if I know, deep down, that person has my best interests at heart.

The main food cop in my early life was my mother. When I got together with Carol, she stepped into the role. I don't think either of us planned it that way or were even conscious of the dynamic at the time. Looking back, though, it seems fairly obvious that we were both staying within familiar patterns of behavior and relating.

Carol had been raised by an older sister. The sister's husband was a fat man who, with the help of or brow-beating by his wife, had taken off a lot of weight and kept it off. Carol, then, had had plenty of close-up education in the job of food cop. As for me, even though I sometimes bristled at the interference, I was accustomed to having an "enforcer" in my life, and in some sense I guess I needed one.

That said, Carol and I, to this day, have issues about food. This is embarrassing to admit. I'm 66 years old. Carol and I have been together for more than four full decades now, and our marriage has been the strongest and most stable component of our lives. You'd think we would have worked out how to deal with each other at table! Yet we still have our little quarrels and quibbles, our moments of resentment and hurt feelings. This testifies, I think, to the depth and power of the emotions that go with food and eating.

There are two sides to every argument, of course. And I suspect that there are millions of otherwise happy couples who fall into sometimes childish bickering over matters of food. To better understand all sides of the question, I've asked Carol to add her own perspective. Here is some of what she has to say.

Okay, this is where I get to defend myself against the charge of being at various times a food cop, an enabler, or even an unwitting saboteur. Seriously, I'm happy for the chance to write about these matters, because they have long been issues for me as well.

I can't separate living with Michael, and living with his obesity, from my own experience with weight management. I come from a family of eaters and am an enthusiastic eater—and sometimes overeater—myself. Back when we were courting, food was a very important part of our bond, a shared passion that helped bring us together. It has occurred to me that I might have married Michael because of the potato salad and rib-eye steak at Charlie's Café Exceptionale or the fondue and baked stuffed eggplant at the Lowell Inn!

But if Michael and I both loved to eat, I seemed to have been luckier in the matter of metabolism. I was thin as a child, and even as a young woman I seemed to burn through as many calories as I could possibly take in. Clearly there was an injustice here: similar behavior led to serious consequences for Michael, but not for me.

Then, as I was approaching 40—and still hoping to be a mother someday—I developed a fibroid tumor in my uterus. This is a benign and fairly common sort of tumor, but since both my mother and my sister had died at young ages of cancer, I reluctantly agreed to the gynecologist's recommendation that I undergo a hysterectomy. One of the implications of the procedure was that I basically went into instant menopause. I also started gaining weight. The reasons for this will never be certain. Perhaps it was because of physical changes or my disappointment at losing my chance to bear a child. I believe I was eating more, and if I was depressed, it was not without cause.

At any rate, as is the case with many women, my whole metabolism seemed to slow down. For the first time in my life, I couldn't just eat whatever I felt like, and I had a tough time controlling my diet. If there's anything good to be said about this, it's that the situation gave me a more intimate under-standing of what Michael had been wrestling with all those years.

As my weight ratcheted up, Michael sometimes expressed feelings of guilt, as though it was his overeating that was making me put on pounds and inches. But I have always felt that my weight gain was caused by these midlife circumstances, not by anything that Michael could do or say.

Unlike Michael, I haven't kept extensive records of my weight. But I can tell you that my dress size has ranged from 8 to 18; in my closet now are clothes from size 12 up. Along the way I've been on many diets—some very sensible ones and some ridiculous fads. I've tried Weight Watchers (more than once), Counterweight, Overeaters Anonymous, Diet Workshop, Atkins, Stillman, Pritikin, the Kelp diet, and Diet Center. I've been on a protein-sparing fast. I've tried a cabbage-soup diet; I've eaten only grapefruit and bananas for several days, followed by days of nothing but tomato juice. Once I ate only steak and deviled eggs for a week.

So then, coming back to the dynamic between Michael and me, it should be clear that there's a lot of history, baggage, and emotion on both sides of the equation.

For a long time I have felt that Michael and I compete with one another. We love each other, but sometimes we seem to act more like siblings than partners. I think many married couples do this some of the time. Even as I think I am being supportive, I compete with him and he competes with me. Maybe that's why we sometimes seesaw in our eating behavior.

I think of this as the "codependent" part of our relationship. Let's say we're eating in a restaurant. Maybe on that particular occasion, Michael is being virtuous. He orders fish, no sauce, and salad, no dressing. Sometimes this makes me more inclined to order a rich, gourmet dish. I feel that Michael is being holier-than-thou; Michael feels I'm digging my grave with a fork. In other words, there are also moments when he plays the food cop.

Things are better when we operate independently. I order what I feel like eating, without regard to what Michael is having. When we're in that mode, we both tend to eat pretty sensibly.

Best of all is when we function interdependently, making shared decisions that work for both of us. For example, I might wait until Michael has ordered, then ask for the same thing or see if there's something he'd like to share. That way, we both end up with something healthy.

These same categories seem to apply when we eat at home. Michael and I both like to cook, but it is more challenging when you limit butter, oil, cheese, prepared sauces, and other good stuff. So, much of our home dining comes down to foraging and improvising with leftovers. Sometimes this is fun and leads to wonderfully creative meals. Sometimes it is chaos.

When we are stuck in codependent mode, I might be aware that Michael is doing very well in managing his eating. And yet I might find myself bringing fattening foods into the apartment— things I know he would enjoy. I don't tell him the food is there. It's for me or for guests. Of course, I don't need the fattening stuff either. I'm not trying to sabotage Michael's efforts to eat well, but the effect is the same. I'm making things more difficult for him. At times he makes things more difficult for me. In a perfect world or between perfect people, I suppose this wouldn't happen. But that's not how life is.

An element of chaos sometimes creeps in when we are operating independently. I try to figure out what Michael might want for dinner. Invariably, he has something else in mind. Not infrequently we prepare our meals separately. We eat together but have different food.

Things are better when we work interdependently. We discuss what we are going to do about meals, the shopping is planned, our eating is better organized and healthier. We still make last-minute decisions, but they are mutual decisions.

I agree with Michael that, after 40 years of essentially a very happy marriage, you might think we'd deal more smoothly with some of these basic issues. The difficulty, I think, comes not from Michael's and my differences but from our similarities. We are both preoccupied with eating; food is at the center of our respective worlds. Sometimes it's hard for us to clearly perceive each other's needs or defer to each other's preferences because we are locked in such similar struggles, prey to the same temptations.

No matter how well I am eating at a given time, I allow myself indulgences, and I try my best to separate my indulgences from Michael's. At the end of the day, what he eats is his business, and what I eat is mine. We cannot watch each other's food. If we do, we compete. If Michael orders something fatty, that is not license for me to do the same, and vice versa.

Let me confess that I hide things from Michael. This is not a difficult confession, since he's probably been aware of it for decades! There are some foods that I like to have around and that he can't tolerate having in the apartment. So I spirit them away. I figure what he doesn't know won't hurt him.

I know he's hiding stuff from me too. That's okay.

We'll probably always have our food issues. Everyone has something. But we really care about each other. And that counts more than calories.

CHAPTER 7

THE HONEYMOON
YEARS

Being young, busy, and far from wealthy, Carol and I took time for only a brief honeymoon—five days in Chicago. By the end of that whirlwind vacation, I'd put on 12 pounds.

Gaining 12 pounds in 5 days is not an easy thing to do. I worked at it. One night we went to a Scandinavian smorgasbord—bad idea!—followed by a marionette show. I ate so much during dinner that by the time we got to the show, I had to loosen my belt and undo the top button of my pants. I'm not sure which was worse, the physical discomfort or the sheer embarrassment.

Looking back, it seems that I was entering a stage when I was leading two different lives. One life was coming to be defined by a gratifying pattern of discovery and success;

the other continued to be a saga of frustration and failure.

False modesty aside, I was proving to be effective in my work, and I was recognized for it. After the 1964 campaign, then Minnesota attorney general Fritz Mondale offered me a job as a lawyer in his office. This was more than just a wonderful opportunity; it was also the beginning of a terrifically important professional and personal relationship. Mondale turned out to be one of the most gracious and sensitive men I have ever met in politics. He had—and has—a ready wit, but never used humor as a way of putting people down or asserting his authority. In a milieu where many people seemed to feel it was okay to make jokes or comments about race, or ethnicity, or sexual orientation, or fatness, Mondale never stooped to such cheap shots. I went on to work for him, in various capacities, for many years, and never once did he make an unkind reference to my size; in fact, he never made *any* reference to it. With my career up and running, my personal life, too, was going well. I'd overcome my early awkwardness with women to make a good and solid marriage. I'd survived the name-calling of childhood and the alienation of adolescence, becoming a reasonably sociable adult blessed with friends and colleagues I respected and enjoyed.

If, as Freud suggested, the requirements for happiness are love and work, I was essentially a happy man. Both personally and professionally, I was living an extended honeymoon.

Then there was my other life—my life as a fat person who had the damnedest time controlling his eating and his weight. In *that* life, I was often helpless and bewildered, disappointed in myself and all too ready to take offense at the attitudes of others. I could hardly feel content or peaceful when that aspect of my existence came to the fore.

Decades later, I would turn to psychotherapy to try to reconcile these two versions of my life; I would learn at last that acceptance of myself as a fat person was the key to making my dual existence whole again.

But in my twenties and thirties I was just muddling through, groping after understanding. My two lives went along in a state of simmering conflict. Would the parts of me that felt competent and capable win out over the part that felt helpless? Could happiness and self-respect survive within the skin of someone who could not stop himself from being fat?

When I think about those years, what strikes me are the contradictions. For example, as a lawyer in the attorney general's office, I was serious and dignified. My persona was defined by the work I did and had little or nothing to do with my size. Still, on weekends, I remained all too inclined to play the jolly fat man.

Carol and I had moved into a suburban apartment complex of primarily younger married couples who tended to hang out together. During the summer the swimming pool became the social center. On Sunday afternoons we held what we called the water follies, in which the residents performed various aquatic exhibitions for each other's amusement. There were divers and prodigious breath-holders, even synchronized swimming.

My contribution was to do spread-eagled belly flops while others took measurements of just how far I could get the water to splash onto the wide apron around the pool. If I arched my back, led with my belly, and made good hard contact with my thighs, I could get a fair-size tsunami going.

Now, there's nothing tragic about this; it was good clean fun. Still, I wonder why I felt compelled to play the clown and to make my size the focus of my clowning. Did I *want* to draw attention to my fatness? Did I want my social identity to be defined first and foremost by my size? My behavior certainly made it seem that way. Probably I was making a kind of preemptive strike—making fun of my fatness before anyone else could do it for me.

In any case, Carol and I soon moved away from that apartment and from Minneapolis. Fritz Mondale had been appointed senator from Minnesota when Hubert Humphrey became vice president. Now, in 1966, he was running for his own term and asked me to work full-time on his campaign. After his victory, he invited me to join his Senate staff. So, two days before Christmas of 1966, Carol and I packed up and headed for Washington, D.C.

For someone with my interests and ambitions, Washington is Mecca, and I was tickled to be going there. But again, as my professional life went well, my "fat life" went badly.

Every business has its customs, and the business of politics is no exception. We all know the cliché of the smoke-filled room. That cliché was on its way out by the 1960s, but other customs were alive and well. Some of these had to do with food. Political types tend to eat a lot of steak; in some ancient and symbolic way, red meat seems to correlate with power. Bigger steak, more power! I'm not sure how the giant baked potatoes and slabs of cheesecake enter into the equation, but suffice it to say that a fair amount of political persuading and schmoozing gets done over big, heavy meals. By November 1967, I was back up to 265 pounds; I'd gained back more than half the weight I took off for the wedding.

In 1968, Hubert Humphrey decided to run for president, and Fritz Mondale was selected to cochair his campaign. Around the first of April I started working full-time to get Humphrey elected.

Among the many things I learned from this first foray into presidential politics was that national campaigns and weight control do not go together. The pace of work too often turns breakfast into a time for doughnuts, dinner into a junk-food orgy. Faced with the stress and the barely controlled chaos of the campaign, my weight kept ratcheting up. When it passed 270, my doctor recommended that I embark immediately on a 1,000-calorie diet. I didn't do it; I didn't even seriously consider it. I'm not saying that my job stress was an adequate excuse for eating badly; that would contradict my belief in personal responsibility. But I will say that, in the context of the madness of campaigning, I found myself powerless to make good choices.

In early June I was assigned to begin preparing the Humphrey campaign operations for the Democratic National Convention, to be held in Chicago. Even before the event itself, Chicago was wild that summer. With the upcoming convention as leverage, telephone workers, bus drivers, and cab drivers had all gone on strike. The city was filling up with people planning massive anti–Vietnam War demonstrations. Mayor Richard Daley was growing increasingly strident and frightening in his rhetoric about maintaining order. Against that frenzied backdrop, I was deeply involved in the logistics of the convention: arranging transportation, securing hotel rooms, setting up communications. Control my eating in those circumstances? Fat chance.

No one who lived through those times can forget the '68 convention—the violence, the bloodied demonstrators, the painful spectacle of a country at war against itself. My professional life afforded me the privilege of a front-row seat to history.

But I also carry away a more private memory of that dramatic summer—a melancholy milestone of my "fat life." In July of 1968, for the first time ever, I weighed more than 300 pounds. When Chicago was over, I tipped the scales at 305.

It occurs to me that in the course of this narrative I have made frequent reference to my eating compulsion but haven't really described what that compulsion *feels* like. I guess I've always assumed that people will know.

Other fat people probably don't need such a description, though chances are that different people experience these cravings in various ways. As for *unfat* people, it's at least possible that they don't really get it. So here, without apology or a whole lot of analysis, is my best shot at describing the role food plays in my life and what it's like to live each day in a world of unending temptations.

The first thing I'd like to say is that, among addictive substances, food is the only one where *just saying no* is not an option. An alcoholic can stop drinking. A cigarette smoker or a person with a drug problem can go cold turkey. I'm not in any way downplaying the pain or difficulties that other kinds of addicts face, but they at least have solutions that are definite, clear-cut, black-and-white. With a food addiction, it's all gray areas. Sure, I can say no to particular foods—no to chocolate, no to ice cream, no to fatty corned-beef sandwiches—but I can't just stop eating altogether. I'm stuck with the slippery, elusive, vague idea of moderation; and, for a person like me, moderation has been the hardest thing in the world.

At a given moment, my eating may or may not have much to do with what most people would describe as "hunger." For that reason, I guess, I've never been able to eat just one of anything. I've already told the story of the 12 Coney Island hot dogs. That episode might have been extreme, but, sadly, it was nothing like unique. Give me a pound of chopped liver and a full sleeve of saltines, and, when I'm in the grip of my compulsion, I will keep eating till the last dollop of liver has been spread across the final cracker. I have been known to eat an entire salami at a sitting, whittling it as I went along, never putting down the knife. At times in my life, a six-egg omelet and two or three bagels have been my idea of brunch.

When I am in that mode, I don't just eat food, I inhale it. Once the food is in front of me, I am obsessively single-minded about eating it and extremely systematic as to how I do so. If there are several items to be eaten, I generally eat all of one before I move on to the next. I start with my least favorite and work toward my most favorite. Like a kid with a piece of birthday cake, I am careful to save the most exquisite bite for last.

If the only food available is something I don't really like, it mysteriously becomes more appetizing, and I eat a lot of it anyway. I like to think I know good food from bad, but I am all too inclined to choose quantity over quality. At times I have treated eating as a demonstration sport. On several occasions, people have offered to keep buying me food, just to see how much I could eat.

But what is it that stimulates my appetite to such extremes? The short answer is: everything.

Maybe more "normal" eaters don't feel this constant tug, but for me the world is one huge shopping cart full of stimulus and temptation. I drive down a city street; it seems like an unending procession of pizzerias, burger joints, and cafés. I can smell a bakery blocks away. I go to the movies; the refreshment stand looms large between me and the auditorium. I can smell the roasting popcorn and the butter sauce. I can almost taste the Milk Duds and Junior Mints, slightly stale but wonderful in their rattling cardboard boxes.

Restaurants drive me to distraction. Waiting to be seated, I watch the trays of food go by. Strolling to my table, I check out what other diners are having. Steaks, lobsters . . . Are they good? Are they *big*? What's that creamy-looking sauce on the pasta? By the time I reach my seat, I am in a state of agitated indecision. That's even before I've glanced at the menu. The menu takes my dilemma to another level. So many dishes, so lovingly, almost erotically described. . . .

It isn't only at mealtimes that I'm preoccupied with

food. I often spend the morning wondering what I'll have for lunch; a big part of my afternoon is anticipating dinner. Exercising, I think about what I'll eat when I am finished. Often, having just completed dinner, I'll find myself wondering what I will have for breakfast.

I once wrote a manual for people organizing political campaigns. In it, I talk about the three times a day for having meetings: breakfast, lunch, and dinner. It was pointed out to me that most people might have said morning, afternoon, and evening. Not me. Without even thinking about it, I divide the day into mealtimes and the spaces between them.

It's understandable, I guess, that my food fixation is an around-the-clock affair, because I look to food for so many different things:

You're feeling blue, you're feeling down? Have something to eat; you'll feel cheerier.

You're under stress? Have something to eat; it will relieve the pressure.

You're looking for something easy and neutral to do with a friend or colleague? Go out for a leisurely meal together.

You're feeling bored? Prepare something interesting to eat.

You're feeling creative? Ditto.

You have a problem that you want to put out of your mind? Eat something tasty and forget about it for a while.

You're proud of something you've accomplished? Reward yourself with something good to eat.

You want to show your love for yourself? Treat yourself to something delicious.

You need something to calm you down? Eat something heavy; it'll make you sleepy.

You're upset with how fat you are? Have something to eat—you'll have a brief moment of escape before getting even more depressed.

Clearly, food is my drug of choice for a wide variety of uses. And let's face it—it's a marvelous drug with a wonderful array of properties. It soothes; it gives pleasure; it's as much of a social lubricant as alcohol, as much of a solace as peaceful sleep; it yields moments of complete euphoria.

The tragedy, of course, is that these benign effects don't last for very long. As with every drug, the high wears off, and then there are dues to be paid, in the form of a following low. As with other drugs, food has side effects.

If you've been eating to reward yourself, that's not so bad; rewards are, by their nature, fleeting. But if you've been eating to conveniently ignore a problem, you find that your fullness wears off but the problem still exists. If the problem happens to be that you are unhappy about being fat, you obviously have made the problem worse. Still, when your drug of choice wears off, what is there to do but take another hit? Or even increase the dosage, in the hope of extending the good feelings just a little longer. Thus overeating encourages even greater overeating.

My eating compulsion is with me always. Moreover, its virulence has not diminished over the years. This, I believe, is one of the hard realities that need to be accepted about the fat disease: The disease itself is tireless; it never flags. Over the whole span of my life, with all my ups and downs of weight, with all my attempts to control my addiction through therapy and education, my desire for food has not really lessened or changed. When I am hungry—whatever that word exactly means to a fat person—I am as hungry as ever.

What *has* changed is that I manage my cravings better than I used to. Not perfectly; not completely, but better. I'm proud of this because I know how difficult it's been to get there.

My disease is with me always—but that's not to say that its influence is constant. It ebbs and flows. There are days when moderation seems almost easy, no big deal. *Of course* I can say no to dessert—what's the problem?

Other days there is a battle going on inside me from the moment I wake up until the time I go to bed again. Some days, even as I fight, I know that I will be defeated, and that defeat will be both humiliating and secretly sweet. Losing the battle means that I will eat the things I crave—and not feel lousy about it till at least a little later.

CHAPTER 8

UNACKNOWLEDGED
CONSEQUENCES

Here is a simple but valuable piece of advice: If you weigh 298 pounds and haven't exercised much for a decade or so, don't try leaping over a tennis net. I learned this lesson the hard way on a Sunday morning in 1972.

Over the previous few years, Carol and I had been shuttling back and forth between Washington and Minneapolis, as my work on Senator Mondale's staff alternated with my running campaigns back at home. My weight had also shuttled up and down, generally in rhythm with the election cycle. During the lulls that followed an election, I usually managed to take off weight; I got down as low as 240 in early 1970. Then the next campaign season would kick in, my eating would spin out of control, and the pounds would come right back. Even though the pattern was more or less predictable, I couldn't seem to break out of it; against my disease, awareness alone was not an adequate weapon.

I promised myself that I would try to live more actively and healthily. Tennis was part of my strategy for that. I really liked the game. It was social, something that Carol and I could do together. I took some lessons, and while it was clear I was never going to Wimbledon, I became proficient enough that I could enjoy myself on the court and begin to get some regular exercise.

Don't ask me what made me think I could jump over the net that day. I guess I'd seen Pancho Gonzales or somebody like that do it once on television. It didn't look so hard! But when I attempted the maneuver, my foot caught on the net cord, my leg twisted into a position for which it hadn't been designed, and I ended up writhing on the court with torn cartilage in my knee.

The irony is that my leap had *re*injured a joint I'd damaged eight years earlier, while attempting—again, don't ask me why—to do a Russian wedding dance. While I may have been physically sluggish most of the time, I did have my moments of rash and exuberant energy, moments when my spirit seemed to be trying to bust out of my fat body, rebelling against the limits imposed by my size. Those moments brought me brief spasms of liberating joy but tended to get me into trouble.

Even though I was in the midst of a campaign, I had no choice but to schedule orthopedic surgery. The procedure went fine but was complicated somewhat by my fatness. And that's the point I'd like to make here: aside from the obvious difficulties that fatness entails, there are a slew of less apparent, indirect, often unacknowledged consequences of being fat. Even when a particular problem has nothing to do with weight per se, fatness has a way of complicating things.

Before my knee surgery, I was given a sedative to prepare me for the spinal anesthesia that was to follow. The sedative made me quite woozy, and as I lay on my side on the operating table, I was only vaguely aware of the anesthesiologist feeling around my lower back. My attention became slightly more focused when I heard the doctor start to curse. Through my haze, I couldn't tell what the problem was. It turned out that, because of my fatness, the anesthesiologist couldn't find the spot where he needed to inject me.

There was a delay, then a brief scuffling. Sometime later I became aware that there were more people in the room. Orderlies. They sat me up on the table, with my legs dangling over the side. Since I was like an extremely large and heavy rag doll at this point, two men had to hold my shoulders as they leaned me forward so I wouldn't fall flat on my face. With my flesh stretched out across my back, the anesthesia could finally be delivered.

If my fatness complicated the prep for my surgery, it made my recuperation more difficult as well. As anyone who's ever injured a knee or an ankle knows, the most important advice is: *keep the weight off it.* Clearly, the more weight you carry, the harder it is to let the injured part rest and heal.

The role of fatness in orthopedic matters is relatively straightforward. But there are other medical issues in which obesity plays a subtler and more mysterious part— a role that, in some instances, is seldom talked about.

Earlier in these pages, my wife, Carol, wrote about how her desire to have a child was thwarted by her need, late in her thirties, to have a hysterectomy. In reality, the story is more complex than that, involving a great deal of emotional pain on Carol's part and a considerable amount of ambivalence and guilt on mine.

For the first six years of our marriage, we practiced birth control; then we decided to let nature take its course. For us, nature's course went nowhere. After about a dozen disappointing menstrual cycles, Carol visited a gynecologist who specialized in matters of fertility. Thus began several years of often embarrassing and physically painful interventions, none of which worked. In the face of Carol's increasing frustration, the gynecologist told us that no one factor dramatically stood out in our inability to conceive, but several factors were marginal. One of these was my sperm count. Fat men apparently have lower counts than unfat men do; this, in turn, seems to be a consequence of the tendency of excess fat cells to inhibit the production of testosterone.

And this raised a number of extremely uncomfortable questions. Was my fatness affecting something as intimate as the capacity to have a child with my wife? Would we have been fertile if I was thinner? Could I have *become* thinner with the conception of a child as a possible reward?

Carol's surgery ended our hopes of conceiving, but even that didn't lay the issue to rest. I was plagued by a kind of simmering guilt, but there was little discussion with Carol about it. At some level, I think I understood the intensity of her pain and felt that the question of her possible resentment would be too unsettling to address. Decades later, as I began working on this book and showing it chapter by chapter to Carol, she noted with surprise that I *still* wasn't talking about the issue of our infertility. This, I think, testifies to the power of the emotions involved. Embarrassment and helplessness had kept me silent. Our inability to conceive was a problem I hadn't been able to fix; since I couldn't fix it, I didn't want to talk about it. For better or worse, that's how most men tend to deal with things, right?

Since fatness has consequences in the most intimate arenas of life, it's hardly surprising that it also complicates things in more public arenas, such as the workplace. Public arenas are where one's own fatness collides with the biases of others—and the results can be highly distressing.

At the end of the 1972 campaign, I decided not to re-join Mondale's staff. Partly, this was because Carol and I had promised ourselves that we would not succumb to "Potomac fever"; we liked Minneapolis and wanted to return. Additionally, now that Mondale had been elected for a second term, he had the luxury of focusing more on policy and less on politics, but politics was what I loved and believed I was good at. I liked the gritty stuff, the warfare.

In any case, back in Minnesota, I now needed a job. An older friend who was a partner in a well-regarded law firm suggested that I meet with him and some of his colleagues. He thought they might be inclined to offer me a position. They were interested in me for legislative and government-related work, and in those fields I had a pretty fair résumé. I'd spent six years with a U.S. senator who'd just been reelected; I'd been closely involved in the campaign of the then-sitting governor.

I dressed carefully for the interviews and had visits with a number of partners. At the end of the day I stopped by my friend's office. It was immediately clear that something had not gone well. My first thought was that they weren't interested in someone without much experience in the conventional practice of law.

I was right—there was a problem. But I was wrong about what it was. My friend was courageously if crushingly candid: the problem was my weight. The partners had been put off by my size; or, rather, they were concerned about how their clients would respond to someone who was so fat. Image was important to them; my image was a big fat minus. My friend was embarrassed and apologetic, but that was that. This was 1972, remember. Employers faced far fewer legal restraints when it came to indulging their biases. And the truth is that even today, except in a few places that clearly define fatness as a disability, fat people have little recourse against prospective employers who reject them because of their size.

I was devastated when I left my friend's office. My fatness had caused me many problems in my life, but this was different. I suppose I was naive, but I'd never really believed that my appearance would hold me back in my career. I was a lawyer and a political operative, after all, not a model or a movie star! And I'd worked so hard *not* to let my fatness limit me. Driven by my determination to be happy and successful in spite of being fat, I'd done a lot to compensate.

I believed then and I believe now that, in some ways, my fatness made me *better* at my work. Self-conscious about my looks, aware that I was starting with a disadvantage, I made a point of being *extra* diligent, *extra* prepared. The same compulsive streak that made me a problem eater gave me an unusual capacity to push myself when confronted by a tough task or a deadline.

All that apparently counted for nothing, as far as these partners were concerned. They took the measure of my silhouette and didn't bother with the rest of me. I won't dwell on the obvious unfairness of this or how furious it made me at the time. If I've learned anything from my decades of living as a fat person, it's that it doesn't pay to get all worked up about the attitudes of others. Being fat was *my* problem. Being prejudiced against fat people was *their* problem. Thankfully, I have outgrown the need to worry about their problem in addition to my own.

In any case, I soon had job offers from equally established firms; I chose to go with a smaller office so that I'd have more freedom to continue pursuing my interest in politics. Over the years, I've worked with many, many clients. To the best of my knowledge, none has had a problem being represented by a fat attorney; none has seen my size as affecting the value of my counsel. I say this because I think it points up a widespread hypocrisy. The partners at the firm that rejected me blamed their own prejudice on some imagined future clients. But the truth is that it was their own bias that they acted on. Their reaction to me was not professional but personal. They were uncomfortable having a fat colleague around.

Again, that's their problem, not mine. Over the years, though, I've been placed in plenty of situations where I couldn't quite deny that my feelings had been hurt or where I felt that some not very funny joke had been made at my expense.

Several years ago, for instance, I was at a Washington party in honor of a good friend who was leaving his job; the party was held in one of those cavernous hotel event rooms. I ran into an acquaintance—a prominent southern senator who never seemed to miss an opportunity to make some purportedly clever remark about my weight. Gesturing around the spacious banquet hall, he said, "I see they got a room that's big enough for you."

Was he just trying to be funny? Was he trying to embarrass me? Was he testing my resourcefulness in an awkward social situation? I worked hard at smiling and mustered as much good nature as I could. "Yes," I said, "and they were even accommodating enough to open up the double doors for me."

Was I wrong to play along with the joke? In that moment, what other choice did I have?

At the end of the 1972 campaign and before I started my new job, my weight was back to 305, equaling my then all-time high. This was bad. My recently repaired knee felt every extra pound. Nearly new clothes already seemed tight. Worst of all, I seemed to be locked into overeating mode, and I saw no way of breaking the upward spiral.

Something radical was called for. I spoke to my doctor about the possibility of a total fast. Since moderation did not seem to be in my repertoire, maybe I should just try to stop eating altogether for a while. The doctor agreed, on the condition that the fast take place in a hospital, where I could be closely monitored. In mid-November, having tacked on one last pound, I checked myself in.

For two weeks I ate nothing. *Nada.* Zilch. How can I describe what a profound and overwhelming change this was? Why not just go without *air* for a couple of weeks? I've spoken about all the many things I use food for: comfort, rewards, alleviating stress or boredom, measuring out the times of the day. Suddenly all of that was gone. I was not only deprived of pleasure but stripped of nearly all my habits and routines. Without the passion and the rituals that went with breakfast, lunch, and dinner, my whole identity became sort of hazy. If I wasn't Mike the Eater, who exactly was I?

During those two weeks, I was the guy who lived on water and vitamins. Without meals to look forward to, the days were excruciatingly flat and uneventful. I watched a lot of television; I read when I could muster the concentration. I exercised with a physical therapist. I chatted with the nurses as they dutifully measured my urine output and checked my blood pressure. I slept as much as I possibly could.

After 14 days of this, I'd dropped 30 pounds. I went home on a diet that started at 800 calories and gradually increased, coming to a more moderate level where, in theory, I could continue losing weight. For a while the strategy worked. I kept shedding pounds, and by mid-1973, I was down to a relatively trim and healthy 243. This was nearly as lean as I'd been on my wedding day, and I felt quite good about it.

Then, in early 1974, I got involved in another political campaign. The stress and habits that went with it brought to the fore something that should have been obvious anyway: I hadn't yet learned to manage my weight in any sustainable way. I lost weight during desperate and contrived episodes that were somehow disconnected from my normal life, using methods that were too extreme to follow for very long. When normal life resumed, the weight came back. This is the classic MO of the yo-yo dieter.

In any case, I agreed to manage the reelection effort of the governor of Minnesota; I also became involved in Walter Mondale's exploration of the possibility of running for president in 1976.

Periodically during 1974, I traveled as an adviser to the

Democratic Senate Campaign Committee. My colleague on these trips was the executive director, a high-spirited and delightful companion. He'd been a pulling guard at Notre Dame in the Knute Rockne era. At this stage of his life, he was quite heavy, in addition to being tall, bull-necked, and broad-shouldered.

He really liked steak. Wherever we traveled, the staff had standing orders to make reservations for us at the best steak house in town. Between the two of us, we made many restaurateurs very happy. It wasn't just the meat we went for. There were also the soft and steaming dinner rolls, the baked potatoes slathered in sour cream and butter. Not that we neglected our vegetables—rich creamed spinach was the classic side dish. Want something light? How about a nice green salad blanketed in Roquefort dressing? But it was the steaks that were the main attraction. Once, at a famous eatery in Tampa that sold steaks by the ounce, I polished off a 40-ounce porterhouse.

By August, not surprisingly, I'd gained back 50 of the 60-something pounds I'd worked so hard to lose; I weighed over 290 again. This was distressing enough, but what was really scary was that the campaign still had over two months to run; the way things were trending, I feared that I would blow right past 300 pounds and just keep going.

It might be useful to note that my weight patterns, not to mention my general stress level, were so profoundly linked to the election cycle, that Carol actually evolved a rather unique way of counting the years of our marriage. "During the odd-numbered years," she says, "between campaigns, Mike was more available and more relaxed and tended to shed pounds. Perhaps we even had a shot at a vacation! During the even-numbered years, Mike tended to disappear into a series of evening meetings that meant pizza, potato chips, hoagies, and hot dogs. In 1979, Mike happened to be traveling with Mondale on Air Force Two on our anniversary. Mondale suggested calling me up. The vice president asked me how long we'd been married. I said seven years. Mondale said, 'Wait a second. I think Mike told me this was your 14th anniversary. 'True,' I said, 'but it's hard to count the even-numbered years.'"

In any case, now desperate to break the momentum, I went back to the hospital for another fast—another brief, unnatural episode. I had a special phone put in my room, saw a lot of visitors, and basically performed my campaign duties from the hospital.

But this second fast didn't last the planned two weeks. It ended early, with disappointment but also with relief.

Frankly, I'd been having a hellish time of it.

After a few days of not eating, I started to hallucinate. Not surprisingly, my hallucinations featured food—especially enormous cheeseburgers. I pictured them with remarkable and almost obscene vividness: I saw the sesame seeds on the bun, the grill marks on the meat through the translucent layer of cheese, the sheen on the blob of ketchup. These unfulfilled fantasies made me irritable and probably a little wiggy. I grew so short-tempered that I hardly recognized myself.

The crisis came around two o'clock one morning. An intern came into my room, told me I'd stopped putting out enough fluid, and announced his intention to insert a catheter into my bladder. I told him there weren't enough orderlies in the hospital to hold me down for that procedure. He told me it was a medical necessity. I told him I'd believe that when I heard it from my own doctor. This led to a standoff, since the intern wasn't about to risk getting screamed at for calling my doctor in the middle of the night.

By the next day my fluid output had picked up, but it was clear that the fast wasn't going well, and my doctor and I agreed that we should end it. I'd lost 23 pounds in 10 days. I went home on the same 800-calorie diet that

I'd used before. I continued to shed some pounds—but not nearly as many as on my first try with this regimen.

This confirmed something that I've noticed again and again over all the years of my attempts at losing weight: a given diet never works as well the second time.

I don't know if there's a physiological reason for this. I do know there's a psychological reason. Human nature being what it is, we badly want to believe that each new diet is a big advance over all the others we've tried, that this is the system that offers the final cure, the lasting solution. Armed with that blind faith, we bring extra motivation to every shiny and well-hyped diet that claims to be a breakthrough.

By the second time we're on that shiny new diet, our faith has been tempered by a dose of reality. It obviously hasn't made us thin forever. It isn't magic, after all; it's only one more variation on what all diets finally come down to: a way of reducing our intake of calories. Beyond the marketing and the hocus-pocus and the mumbo jumbo, that's what every diet is about.

A lasting solution, then, doesn't reside in this or that set of interchangeable buzzwords or recipes or rules. A lasting solution can only come from within ourselves— from an honest assessment of what we're up against and an ongoing and consistent effort to deal with it.

I think we all know that, deep down. Yet hope is a stubborn thing, and nothing is more seductive than the dream of a miracle cure. No matter how many different diets have ultimately disappointed us, we still buy into the fantasy. Maybe this *next* diet will contain the silver bullet, will capture that elusive magic.

And if not the next one, then certainly the one after.

CHAPTER 9

DIETING AT
THE WHITE HOUSE

A t Christmastime of 1977, I had the rare distinction
of being photographed with the vice president
of the United States sitting on my lap. The vice
president's wife was also sitting on my lap. I was wearing
a Santa Claus outfit at the time, complete with fake white
beard and floppy red hat. I was the official vice-presidential Santa. I needed no padding to fill out the suit, and I
loved the job for other reasons as well. Santa made
everyone happy. Even for adults, Santa brought back the
pleasantest of childhood memories.

That same April, I'd been the Easter Bunny. I'd had my
picture taken dressed up as a giant, rotund rabbit, being
chased down a hill at the vice-presidential residence by a
cluster of young children.

I suppose I was still playing the jolly fat man, but at least I was doing it in pretty rarefied surroundings now. My double life—confident and capable out in the world, frustrated within my own skin—was continuing. If anything, the two aspects of it moved even farther apart as my career path ascended.

In the spring of 1976, I'd taken on the job of scheduling the plenary sessions of the Democratic National Convention. When Fritz Mondale was selected as Jimmy Carter's running mate, it was decided that I would go to Atlanta to work at the Carter/Mondale headquarters. I gained weight during the campaign, of course, on my usual election-season diet of junk food and steaks.

Carter and Mondale emerged victorious, and I was asked to join the administration as the vice president's counsel and deputy chief of staff. Carol and I moved back to Washington, and I settled into my workplace at the old Executive Office Building. I was very proud that this same suite had once been occupied by Teddy Roosevelt and later by Franklin Roosevelt, when each of them had worked at the Department of the Navy.

Through the mid-1970s, my weight had continued to yo-yo; I'd been on a number of diets and hadn't stuck with any of them for very long. It is perhaps worth mentioning that I was on the Atkins diet way back in 1975. It's strange to me that, at the start of the new millennium, Atkins became such a huge culture-rocking fad; this was a case of fresh buzz attaching to a pretty old idea. Even in the 1970s, there were other low-carb, high-fat diets being hyped. Remember the Royal Canadian Air Force diet? I was on that one, too. On both those regimens I dropped some pounds—and my cholesterol headed for the moon.

In July of 1977, with the pressures of campaigning temporarily over and my weight hovering in the low 290s, I decided to make a concerted effort to get less fat. I enrolled at the Diet Center franchise in our neighborhood. This was to be the most successful episode of weight reduction I'd had so far.

There were many things I liked about the Diet Center's approach. There was nothing gimmicky or weird about the system—no only-tomatoes-every-third-day kind of craziness. They just suggested limiting calories and avoiding certain foods that were obviously fattening. To encourage self-awareness, they asked you to keep records of what you ate. They also encouraged weekly visits with counselors, who were themselves successful veterans of the program.

But perhaps the most refreshing and valuable aspect of the Diet Center approach was this: they stressed that being fat was not exclusively a function of what you ate but of how you lived. Fatness, in other words, was not just some characteristic that happened to attach to you but an integral part of who you were.

This rang very true to me. It covered things like my lifelong tendency to look to food for comfort and stress reduction. It certainly spoke to my sedentary habits and longstanding aversion to taking regular exercise. Doing my damnedest to get with the program, I tried to alter not just my eating but my life. I started jogging.

The results were immediate and, frankly, pretty impressive. Though I huffed and puffed at first, and though my knees and ankles sometimes hurt, the weight came melting off. I found it relatively easy to stick to the diet, in part because I was eating breakfast and lunch six days a week at the White House mess—a private dining room, located on the ground floor of the White House, reserved for those who worked there. In the collegial atmosphere of the mess hall, I could order very carefully, with no embarrassment or qualms about the occasional special request; and there was a big salad bar from which I usually selected my lunch.

I recently found a copy of a note I sent to my doctor after half a year on the Diet Center program. In light of the backsliding and the struggles that were still to come, I find this message poignant if not heartbreaking, but it's an accurate reflection of my frame of mind at the time:

Dear Dr.—,

Today, January 9th [1978], marks six months and I have lost 62 pounds. I have a faint suspicion that this time I may make it.

P.S. This is more weight than I have ever lost on a single diet.

Things continued to go well, and by April I had shed 74 pounds. I weighed 217. I won't say I was willowy, but consider this: At the age of 39 I weighed less than at any time since I was 16 years old—almost 20 pounds less than when I'd graduated high school! I don't mind saying that I thought I looked pretty good. And I felt terrific— physically strong and unabashedly proud of myself.

Then, while jogging one day, I pulled a hamstring. The injury was painful but not particularly serious, certainly not uncommon; everyone who exercises pulls a muscle now and then. But while I was recuperating, something happened. It was as if the break in my routine also broke the spell; as soon as my new healthy habits paused, old habits clawed their way back in. My leg healed fine, but I didn't go back to jogging.

I started gaining weight immediately. At first the gains were minimal, and I could tell myself they were insignificant; I was still in a pretty good range. But if I ever really believed that, I was kidding myself. For me, *any* weight gain was significant, and here's why: just as moderation was incredibly difficult for me, so was *holding steady* with my weight.

I have heard of people who weigh basically the exact same thing for years, even decades, on end; to me, this is nothing short of miraculous. Until recently, my weight almost *never* stayed the same, even for several months at a stretch. At a given time, I was either gaining or losing, losing or gaining, in a relentless and somewhat exhausting pendulum swing. If I allowed a gaining trend to get even slightly established, I had nowhere to go but up until the trend had run its course.

On my 40th birthday, in April 1979, I weighed 240. This was only five pounds heavier than on my wedding day; still, there were signs that trouble was brewing, that my eating was once again threatening to spin out of control. On several occasions, I responded defensively and angrily when Carol played the food cop. In answer to even mild criticism, there were episodes when I threw food in the garbage or stormed out of the kitchen. It seems clear to me now that the disproportion of my reactions was based on guilt and helplessness.

I don't blame external pressures for my gains in weight, but stress sure didn't make life any easier. When Carter/Mondale lost the 1980 election, I took on the rather melancholy chore of managing the vice president's transition out of office. The transition was a personal one as well; it marked the end of what was by far the most exciting job I'd had up to that point and probably one of the most interesting jobs that anyone could ask for. I'd traveled to Israel, Egypt, Portugal, Spain, the former Yugoslavia, Austria, and London. I'd attended meetings with the president. I'd been responsible for overseeing all legal and ethical matters that pertained to the vice president and his staff and for navigating the treacherous waters where such concerns intersected with practical politics.

With that experience under my belt, I joined a D.C. law firm—again, a wonderful opportunity, but full of the challenges and pressures that go with any new job. I also helped out on various congressional campaigns and began working on a political action committee organized by Mondale supporters. When the "Mondale for President" campaign got going in January 1983, I was its treasurer.

By that time, my weight was up to 309—a new all-time high. Realizing that I'd better do something to reverse the upward trend, I went back to the Diet Center. True to past experience, the program didn't work as well the second time. I dropped 15 or 20 pounds, then stopped. The upward spiral soon resumed. By August 1983, with both the campaign and my compulsive eating in full swing, I was up to 316, with no top limit in sight.

In October I entered a weight-management program at a local hospital. I met regularly with a therapist/counselor, worked on behavior modification, and followed a quite strict diet. The program called for several days a week at 700 calories a day; the other days allowed for 1,200 to 1,500 calories.

Another feature of the program was very detailed record-keeping. You were supposed to write down everything you ate, as well as every bit of exercise you did. Not only that, but you were supposed to keep a journal that would track how you felt, both physically and emotionally.

I did quite well in the early stages of this program. The weight was coming down; I felt hopeful once again. Then the record-keeping became too time-consuming and annoying. And I quit.

The patterns of a life emerge only gradually. It's hard to see them until they've been repeated a few times and the essential theme can be distinguished from the incidental variations. Looking back, one such pattern now seems pretty clear: I've been quite consistently resourceful and ingenious at coming up with excuses for quitting weight-loss programs.

One pulled muscle cured me of jogging. Why? I felt good about the exercise and the results I was seeing. I could have resumed when my hamstring healed. But I had an excuse for not doing so, so I didn't.

Another time it was the record-keeping that bothered me—that gave me a legitimate-sounding reason to abandon a program that otherwise was working for me. But if keeping notes and jotting down my feelings bothered me so much, why would I be writing this book? No, the aversion to record-keeping was just a convenient pretext for abandoning a diet.

If I found excuses for quitting weight-loss programs

because they were going badly, that would at least be readily understandable. But in fact the opposite is true. On at least several occasions I have dropped out of programs just when they were going *well*. It's as if I scared myself with the possibility that at some point I actually might not be fat anymore.

That may seem perverse, but I can tell you that the subconscious fear is real and powerful and is one of the reasons that people quit successful diets. It's also part of the reason that people who have dropped a lot of weight tend to put it on again.

The concept is known as fat dependence. I'd heard the phrase for years before I really understood it. I used to think it was more or less the same thing as food dependence; in fact, it's a very different notion. Food dependence deals with the present moment: What do I need right now? Why do I look to food to fill that need?

Fat dependence, by contrast, deals with deeper, more intimate, more lasting issues. What does being fat do for me? What other problems does my fatness mask? From what other concerns and anxieties does being fat distract me?

Fat is something you can hide behind. Fat can be a figurative as well as a literal insulator. Even for people who consciously long to be thin, the prospect of facing life without that insulation can be subconsciously terrifying. This dynamic was neatly summed up in a recent study of the high dropout rate among successful dieters: "It turned out," went the conclusion, "that for many of these people, weight was not a problem. It was a solution."

A solution for what? That varies with the individual, of course. But a classic example would be using fatness as a "solution" for the anxieties that go with being sexually available. By making oneself fat—and therefore conventionally unattractive—a person can remove him- or herself from situations that are too uncomfortable to deal with more directly.

Speaking for myself, I have to acknowledge that I have used my fatness for many things and have thereby kept myself trapped in a very basic paradox: I don't like being fat, but the thought of *not* being fat has been, for most of my life, as unsettling as it is appealing.

I have written earlier about the unsatisfactory social life I had in high school. The bottom line is that girls didn't want to date me because I was fat. This didn't make me happy, yet at the same time it settled some normal adolescent anxieties. At least I knew why I wasn't popular in the boy-girl arena. It was simple; it was clear. I didn't have to look any further or deeper for things about myself that people might not like. Once I got accustomed to being a guy that girls liked to talk to but not go out with, that role became relatively comfortable, something I could handle. What if I got thin and still didn't pass muster as dating material? What would I blame it on then? It was easier not to have to face that question.

In other ways, too, I sometimes think I have used my fatness as a way of limiting my social contacts, again as a way of insulating myself. I like people and I cherish my friends, but in many ways I am essentially a loner. Outside of my professional role, in many situations I can be shy. My fatness reinforces this, in some way seems to justify it. Self-conscious about my size, I have a handy pretext for retreating from more company than I really want. Limited in my physical capabilities, I have a reason to say no to situations or activities that make me anxious or uncomfortable. I don't have to do a lot of difficult and possibly painful soul-searching about why I don't always feel sociable or why I'm not more physically adventurous; I have a simple answer. It's because I'm fat.

Not that I depend on my fatness only in negative ways. Insofar as dependence can ever be positive, there are also positive aspects to the ways I use my size.

Back in my youth, when I was first discovering some of the strategies that would allow me to be reasonably happy and successful in spite of being fat, my size was a crucial element in defining my identity. I suppose you could say that my size was both the problem and the solution. If it held me back from having a more "normal" social life, it conferred on me a presence and a recognizability that offered other benefits. My size, in an odd way, was what suited me to be the head of the cheerleading squad. It made me a natural for certain theater roles. In other activities such as debating, my fatness seemed to give me a certain authority. Is it just a coincidence that people speak of words or arguments as "having weight?" Why is a weak argument "taken lightly?" My fatness suggested seriousness and solidity.

These are advantages that have carried over into my professional life. In my legal and political work, I don't have to be pretty; I *do* have to make an impression, to convey a sense of gravitas and reliability. People of my volume, especially if they happen to have bald heads and mustaches, tend to be remembered and taken seriously. I don't mind admitting that I have leaned on these advantages, and they have served me well.

But let's come back to the other side of the paradox: I don't like being fat. Being fat is bad for my health and limits me in many ways. For almost my entire life I have wanted to be thinner. And I've had to learn that, if there was to be any real chance of that happening in a lasting way, I would need to do more than just temper my dependence on food. I would need to deal with fat dependence too.

I would need to get rid of my reliance on fat itself— and this has been one of the great challenges of my adult life. I would need to find the nerve to shrug off that comfortable but unhealthy part of my identity. I would need to develop the confidence to face the world without my layer of padding—without my insulation. I would have to dare to have thinner skin.

CHAPTER 10

HITTING BOTTOM

During the frenzied months between the Democratic convention in July 1984 and the election that followed in November, I had a small freezer installed in my campaign office. The freezer was there for one single purpose: to hold the ice cream I could not stop spooning down.

That fall I was completely consumed by work, worry, and probably the most dramatic stint of overeating I'd ever been through. I'd get to my desk around seven in the morning, and I'd sit there—talking on the telephone, hosting various meetings—until well into the night. I got no exercise and precious little fresh air. Unfortunately, my lack of physical activity did nothing to damp my appetite. I seemed to need more and more food to deal with the ever-mounting tension.

Not only was my eating out of control, but I was also tormented by an outbreak of *another* compulsion—one that had bothered me sporadically since childhood but had not been a problem in recent years.

This other compulsion was an irresistible urge to scratch myself. There had been times when, in response to a real or imagined itch on my arms or legs, I started scratching and simply couldn't stop. I scratched myself till I bled. I'd given myself sores that lasted weeks or even months. I scratched myself in my sleep. Sometimes, as a youngster, I wore cotton gloves to bed so that I wouldn't lacerate myself during the night.

During past episodes, my scratching problem seemed most likely to surface when I was working hardest to control my weight—as if one compulsion seized the opportunity to emerge when my attention was focused on beating back the other. When I was giving in to my appetite, I didn't seem to need to scratch. I "solved" stress by eating.

But now no single compulsion seemed adequate to dispel the tension I was feeling. I had the double whammy. I ate *and* I scratched. My legs became so raw that my doctor instructed me to coat them each morning with antiseptic and wrap them in bandages, which I wore all day long.

Meanwhile, at the height of the media blitz that accompanies presidential campaigns, I found myself avoiding TV interviews and declining invitations to appear on various shows—I just felt too self-conscious about how I looked. I didn't want the world to see how fat I'd gotten. *I didn't want to see how fat I'd gotten.* If this was partly vanity, it was also partly shame and maybe the beginnings of fear. I didn't want to confront what I'd been doing to myself.

Fritz Mondale lost the election, and Ronald Reagan swept into a second term. If the end of the campaign put a stop to the tension and the crazy hours, it ushered in an inevitable letdown and exhaustion—the sort of low-grade malaise that tends to follow any spurt of peak effort, especially when all that effort ends in a defeat. Recognizing that I badly needed a dose of R&R, some friends kindly lent us their house on St. John, and Carol and I headed for the Caribbean.

Emotionally as well as physically beat up, I found that I'd become hypersensitive even to small frustrations. On our first day on the island, I was driving up and down steep hills in a car with a stick shift I was not accustomed to. As I neared a summit, gears ground, the car sputtered and lurched, and I stalled. At other times I might have laughed at the sort of slapstick difficulty I was having.

That day I saw nothing funny about it. I pulled to the side of the road and got out of the car. I stood there and I couldn't even speak. I'm not sure I have ever felt more miserable and helpless. Standing there next to the car, I started to cry. I said to Carol that we were going back to the house and not leaving it for the rest of the trip. Fortunately, Carol was in a more reasonable frame of mind than I. She heard me out, then proposed a simple solution: we'd exchange the car for one with an automatic transmission.

Still, I had an awful time that week. I couldn't relax even in a beach chair under the palm trees. I felt too lousy to relax. With the election over, I had nothing to distract me from the problem of my weight; I thought about it all the time. I didn't *do* anything about it; I just brooded. Meanwhile, my body rebelled at almost any form of exercise. A short walk in the sand made my knees and ankles hurt. Wading in the ocean drained me.

Home again in Washington, I didn't feel much better. I weighed 330 pounds—a new high and then some. Carol told me I looked green. I couldn't walk a block without feeling like I'd run a race. A flight of stairs might as well have been a wind sprint. Standing on my feet for any length of time was enough to make my back ache.

I was wearing a size 58 suit by then. I was regularly consuming four or five pounds of red meat a week, along with a dozen or eighteen eggs. It was not unusual for me to wolf down two pounds of chocolate almond bark at a sitting. As for the ice cream, I can't even give an honest estimate of how much I was eating.

Friends started noticing what a bad state I was in. One of them wrote me a loving letter suggesting that, now that the election was over, I might stop trying to organize others and organize myself. That observation pretty much nailed it. My profession consisted, essentially, of fostering order and logic in the political arena; how had my own little life become such a mess?

With my lungs squeezed under so much weight and my belly often overfull when I went to bed, I developed sleep apnea. For those who have never experienced it, this is a rather terrifying phenomenon. Basically, your body forgets to breathe while you're asleep. You lie there as if dead until you're critically out of oxygen, then some reflex fires and you wake up, heart racing, in a momentary gasping panic.

In the face of the apnea, and my greenish pallor, and my ever-diminishing stamina, something positive finally happened: I got scared.

I should have gotten scared sooner, of course. Carol and some of our friends had been scared for a while on my behalf. But denial is a powerful thing, and I'd been imagining that I was still in control, that I could pull out of the tailspin at any time. To preserve that illusion, I basically disallowed conversation. Carol would later tell me that she worried about my health nearly every time I became embroiled in a campaign, but that my behavior made her feel that any mention of my weight was counterproductive. I wouldn't acknowledge how bad things were until they got *really* bad. I had to hit bottom.

This notion of bottoming out applies to many kinds of addiction or other destructive behaviors; it generally takes a crisis to get somebody into rehab. But as painful as it is, the fact of hitting bottom also speaks of resilience and hope; where there *is* a bottom there is also the will and the ability to get a grip and bounce back from the depths. I began to get control of my overeating only when I finally accepted that I was no longer talking about gaining or losing some number of pounds; I was talking about saving my own life.

Some radical change was called for, and the most drastic thing I could think of—short of surgery, which I didn't want—was to enroll at the Pritikin Longevity

Center. Pritikin was based in California, but they had a satellite facility at Downington, Pennsylvania, quite convenient to D.C. I signed on for a two-week residential program beginning in mid-December of 1984.

On the appointed day, I threw some exercise clothes and casual wear into a suitcase and headed for Downington. But, true to my compulsive tendencies and my state of mind at the time, I had to treat myself to one last fling. I stopped at Wagshal's Delicatessen, just a few blocks from my apartment, for a corned-beef sandwich. Then I decided, what the hell, it would be nice to have something to nibble on for the drive. I bought an enormous chunk of pickled tongue, probably two pounds, and I ate it like a candy bar as I drove down the highway—toward the place that I hoped and prayed would make me healthy.

My strongest first impression of Pritikin was of the tidy cluster of resuscitation equipment—defibrillators, oxygen tanks, and such—in the center of the exercise room. Treadmills, stationary bicycles, and other aerobics machines lined the walls. If you had a heart attack, stopped breathing, or turned blue, help was just a couple of steps away.

Pritikin was not a fat farm—in fact, most of my coresidents were of average weight or only slightly heavier. The program had been designed for people with various forms of heart disease or hypertension. Insofar as those problems tended to correlate with fatness, weight loss was a consideration, but a secondary one.

And this, I think, was good for me; it played against my tendency to become obsessed with numbers on a scale. It moved me toward a transition that I believe was an important one, to which I will be making reference throughout the balance of this book: toward thinking less about pounds and more about health; less about weight and more about well-being. I was beginning to understand that if I lived more wisely and more healthily, then weight loss would naturally follow. To put it a slightly different way: I was starting to think less about dieting and more about managing my fatness.

At the time of my entry physical, I weighed 332 pounds. My blood pressure was 155/110 and my cholesterol was 248. I was given a cardiac stress test at a quite low level of activity; the test needed to be cut short after six minutes because I was out of breath and my heart rate was getting dangerously high. The doctor, in a masterpiece of understatement, noted on my chart that "marked physical deconditioning is present." The primary diagnosis was "morbid obesity," with a secondary diagnosis of hypertension.

I began an eating regimen that was about as low fat as one could have—lots of vegetables and grains, very small amounts of fish and chicken, virtually no dairy, and no red meat whatsoever. I eased into an exercise program that consisted mainly of walking and lifting light weights. My waking hours were filled with classes—classes on low-fat cooking, stress reduction, and lifestyle changes.

At the end of two weeks, I had dropped 15 pounds. In the grand scheme of things, this was a tiny loss—less than 5 percent of my weight. Yet I already felt 100 percent better—and this was part of my realization that, at the end of the day, it was health, not pounds, that mattered. My stamina had improved substantially. My coloring was better. My cholesterol had already dropped below 200; my blood pressure was down to 128/88. This was real progress.

I went home with a serious commitment to both the diet and the exercise program. I began walking at least 30 minutes on most days, eventually building up to a point where I was walking three or four miles six days a week.

One day I walked seven and a half miles to a friend's house—which might have been fine if I hadn't had to walk back home again. This bit of excess cost me several days of sore feet and aching knees, yet I was exhilarated to realize that I could make such a trek if I set my mind to it. I was busting out of my limitations.

I stayed in touch with one of my Pritikin doctors and kept him posted as to my progress. In January I proudly wrote to him that "I am successfully holding myself to 1,000 calories or less a day. I still find the food rather dull, but it's tasting a little better. . . . It is now one month in which I have not had any red meat and only minor amounts of any kind of meat. I've made a substantial cut in dairy and haven't added salt to anything."

In March, having lost 54 pounds, I encountered a very familiar obstacle. "The weight loss has slowed down," I wrote the doctor, "but each time I get anxious because I don't seem to have lost anything for a few days, it drops another pound or two. . . . I've avoided all the no-no's."

By June I could report that "I've lost 87 pounds, three inches around my neck and nine or ten inches at the waist. The only 'cheating' I've done is, on occasion, to run the calories up to 1,500—but only with permitted foods. It's been six months now and I have not touched red meat, pastries or ice cream, fried foods, sugar-based foods, etc."

Then, in August, I had the pleasure of informing the doctor that a long-awaited milestone had been reached. "I promised a progress report when I'd lost 100 pounds. Actually, I'm down 103! My waist has gone from 58 to 44. My latest blood test shows my cholesterol at 175."

In December I went back to Downington for a one-week refresher course. By that time I'd lost 112 pounds—nearly 35 percent of my total weight at my high. At 172, my cholesterol was well within the acceptable range. I took another stress test; this time it was no problem. I weighed 220 pounds—still fat by most people's standards, but who cared? Letting go of "most people's standards" was one of the things I'd been working on. I didn't have "most people's" body or "most people's" metabolism or "most people's" appetite; I was trying to deal realistically with the hand I'd been dealt, and the point was that I felt good and I was proud of what I'd been able to accomplish.

I felt so good, in fact, that I agreed to be interviewed and photographed for a D.C. magazine that was doing an article on people who'd dropped large amounts of weight. During the 1984 campaign, remember, I had avoided TV appearances and cameras like the plague; now I was happy to be seen and to talk about what I'd been through and learned in the past year. Who knows— maybe part of my motivation in going public was the hope of creating a situation such that I *couldn't* let myself go again, because it would just be too embarrassing. In any case, I was happy to talk about the lifestyle adjustments that I'd made.

I'd made exercise a regular and even (somewhat) pleasurable part of my routine, rather than being just an occasional drudgery or penance. I'd given up red meat— formerly the keystone of my diet. I'd cut way back on salt and practically given up sugar; sweetness, for me, came only from fruit.

Perhaps the most surprising part was that I'd actually gotten to like the new way I was eating. I saw delicious possibilities in complex carbohydrates such as beans and rice. I found that baked potatoes had a wonderful earthy flavor without the sinful add-ons. Vegetables tasted vivid and distinctive when simply steamed in defatted broth.

Bottom line, I was just plain living better, and the fact that I had lost a lot of weight seemed almost incidental when compared to the realization that I had formed a whole new set of more reasonable, healthier habits.

A happy story. And I wish I could report that it marks the final triumphant chapter in my struggles with fatness and with compulsive overeating. It doesn't, of course. As I've said before, it is my belief that obesity is a chronic disease, an ailment to be managed, not cured. My year on Pritikin was a particularly successful episode of managing. Even more important, it was a big step forward in *learning* how to manage.

But I was still a fat person, prone to behaviors that keep people fat. There would still be times when I would fall back into my lifelong game of sneaking food, times I would concoct almost any excuse for shirking exercise. There would be periods when cravings would irresistibly take over, and I'd backslide into a regimen of steaks and chocolate and megacaloric treats from my beloved delicatessens. I'd gain back most of the weight I'd lost; I'd take it off again, then watch it return yet another time. Many more years would pass before I truly tamed my yo-yoing.

I will say this, however: I have never again weighed 332 pounds, and I am confident that I never will. I have never abused my body or gambled with my health as recklessly as I did in 1984. If my time on Pritikin was not the final fix, it was at least a watershed, a pivotal experience whose benefits are still with me.

I was 45 when I went into the program—and I don't think it's a coincidence that I reached that watershed just at midlife. Priorities shift as we get older.

It occurs to me that fat people—and probably unfat people too—put in a certain number of years just trying to get comfortable in the world and inside their own skins. By my midforties, I had met and mostly overcome those challenges.

I was no longer the fat kid who got teased, the fat teenager who couldn't get a date; I was a happily married man with a caring circle of friends and colleagues. Professionally, I had experienced bias and determined that I wouldn't let it hold me back; I had the career that was right for me, and I had the satisfaction of believing that it counted for something in the world. My fatness still bothered me, sure. But if I stepped back from my preoccupation with my weight, I had to acknowledge that, by some combination of struggle and luck, I'd arrived at a fulfilling and mostly happy life.

There were plenty of challenges up ahead—but they were a quite different set of challenges. I was getting to the age when reasonable people start thinking less about social worries and more about taking care of their bodies.

Fatness complicated many things; it would also compli-
cate the normal issues that go with getting older. Armed
with what I'd learned at Pritikin—and also with my
growing determination to feel as good as I could feel and
live as long as I could live, fat or otherwise—I set out on
that next stage of my life.

PART 3

SOME THINGS I'VE LEARNED

CHAPTER 11

THE SAGA OF MY SUITS

So then, I like to think that, by midlife, I had learned some things. Among them: that my fatness needn't hold me back from personal fulfillment and professional success; that the special problems that went with being fat called for solutions that, in turn, demanded vigilance, honesty, and just plain hard work; that, while weight itself was certainly an issue if not an obsession, it was health and well-being that finally mattered.

The trick now would be to apply these lessons, and others, to the life that I was living day to day—a life that, as I've said, had been strangely divided. Confident and successful in certain arenas, I'd remained frustrated and at times helpless in regard to my fatness. With the aid of things I'd learned and whatever maturity I'd gained, I now faced the challenge of healing that divide.

One of the things I'd learned was that I'd always looked to food for *way* too many benefits, from comfort to stress reduction to my reward of choice. Turning to food was my default mode; I knew that I should try to change that.

So when, after losing all the weight with Pritikin, I decided to give myself a treat, I made sure to make it a very different sort of reward—one that would reinforce my weight loss and my healthier choices rather than working against those things.

I went out and ordered myself three custom-made suits.

I have mentioned earlier in these pages that, fat or otherwise, I am not exempt from occasional spasms of vanity. Earlier in my life, I actually wore a hairpiece for a while; for decades I took pride in my mustache, then shaved it off when its whiteness made me look too old. I happen to like nice clothes. But shopping for them—as every fat person probably knows—had generally been a nightmare.

If I shopped at "regular" stores, I faced the problems of bad to nonexistent selection, as well as the possibility of unpleasantness and condescension from the staff; in one particularly annoying incident at a prominent brand-name store, a snooty salesman approached me and, before I'd even said what I was looking for, informed me they had nothing in my size except scarves and maybe gloves. If, on the other hand, I stuck with the "big and tall" shops, I had only a handful to choose from—although this situation has improved, as manufacturers have grasped the fact that fat people constitute a lucrative and growing market. In any case, shopping for clothes had generally been an occasion for anxiety and frustration rather than pleasure.

This mention of vanity and shopping leads me to a brief aside. There are many wrong, hurtful, and infuriating stereotypes about fat people. To name just a couple: that they lack willpower; that they are lazy. A similarly misguided perception is that fat people don't care how they look. The logic here is that if fat people cared how they looked, they wouldn't let themselves be fat. The glaring flaw in this argument, of course, is that there's a world of difference between *caring* about how one looks and *being happy* with how one looks. Of course fat people care how they look. If anything, fat people might be more concerned about their appearance than unfat people, because added to the normal regard for one's looks is the sometimes pained awareness of other people's attitudes and responses.

But back to my suits.

For most of my adult life, even in professional situations, I'd generally dressed relatively informally. I wore ties no more often than I had to and favored sport coats over suits. I enjoyed having my own style, and, frankly, I believe it served me well. Along with my volume and my baldness, my unorthodox way of dressing made me distinctive.

But there was also another side to my shunning of usual business attire. If I dressed like everybody else, I could more readily be *compared* to everybody else. And I feared I wouldn't look as neat and natty in a business suit as did the other men around me. To put it another way, some people use conformity to mask their personal insecurities; I seemed to use *non*conformity. So I must have been feeling pretty good about myself if I was willing to be seen as one more D.C. lawyer in a three-piece suit.

I went to a tailor who'd done work for me over the years, generally fine-tuning the dimensions of rented tuxedos in a wide range of sizes. Now he took careful measurements at the neck, chest, waist, hips, and thighs. Then I had the pleasure of picking out the fabrics; I went for pinstripes in gray, blue, and brown. The bill was $2,100—a lot of money in 1986, but what the hell, I'd earned a little luxury.

Custom clothing doesn't happen overnight; about 10 weeks passed before my suits were ready. When I was called in for the final fitting and saw the suits arrayed on overlapping hangers, I felt that they were worth the wait. The fabric was beautiful; the cut was elegant. They were gorgeous suits.

But they didn't fit. The jackets pulled across my back. The vest buttons tugged at the buttonholes. The trousers were too snug in the waist and seat. I asked the tailor if there'd been some error. It was a hopeful question but a disingenuous one; I knew the answer. The suits were as measured; the truth was I'd been gaining weight. In the time it took to have them made, I'd already outgrown my beautiful new clothes.

The tailor let out the waists of the pants. There was nothing to be done about the vests and jackets. I took the suits home and stuck them in the closet; they hung there accusingly, waiting for the day when I would drop these freshly gained pounds so I could wear them.

What had been going on during those weeks and months when I started putting on weight again? The honest answer is: nothing much. It was a quiet part of the election cycle, and I was under no special stress. I wasn't bingeing on ice cream or steaks. But, by almost imperceptible degrees, my vigilance and discipline had been slipping; ever so gradually, I'd been falling away from the careful eating habits that had worked so well.

It was a subtle process—maybe I had some cheese and crackers here, a brisket sandwich there—but it generated its own momentum. Each extra pound made exercising a bit more of a chore; I found reasons to skip a day now and then. Skipping exercise, in turn, meant I burned up fewer calories and paid the price for every extra bit of eating. And so the cycle went.

I'd learned some things, yes, and certain things I *hadn't* learned; not yet, at least. One of these was the knack of holding steady at a given weight. At that stage of my life, if I wasn't losing, I was gaining. It was one or the other, and I honestly can't say why this was. Was it just my physiology? An inevitable sort of diet fatigue? Fat dependence asserting its grip? Chances are it was all of the above.

For a while my gaining was extremely gradual, and I told myself I could reverse the trend at any point. The only problem was I didn't. By May of 1988, I had gained back 35 pounds and was tipping the scale at 255. But the steep part of the gaining curve was still to come.

Nineteen eighty-eight was an election year; in late summer I went to Boston to work with the Democratic presidential candidate, Michael Dukakis. I'd liked and admired Dukakis ever since we'd first met, in 1984. At that time, he was governor of Massachusetts and also on Mondale's short list of possible vice-presidential candidates. One morning I went to interview the governor at his home—a perfectly ordinary house in a perfectly ordinary neighborhood. But what really impressed me was that, at 7 A.M., Dukakis was out mowing his own lawn.

In any case, as the campaign season advanced, my weight once again advanced alongside it. I was swept out of the routines that had kept my fatness relatively stable. I was far away from the YMCA where I'd walked the track or ridden an exercise bike. I was away from Carol, my food cop. I was once again among the political types who really liked their steaks, once again in a pressure-cooker atmosphere that I couldn't seem to cope with except by eating excessive quantities of food. From early morning till late at night, I worked in a small cubicle filled with jangling phones and frantic staff. State campaign managers came in pleading for more of the candidate's time. Speechwriters demanded more details of each scheduled appearance; meanwhile, the appearances were being constantly reshuffled. This was multitasking to the limit.

My new knowledge faced off against a lot of old temptations. The old temptations won. With meetings at breakfast, lunch, and dinner, plus a few more in between, I was basically eating five or six meals a day. Campaign offices are always stocked with candy and other goodies for the helpers; I ate my share and more. By the end of the campaign I weighed 280. Worse, I had regressed into destructive habits. Steak houses and delis lured me in. I resumed my old game of hiding food in the apartment, eating it when Carol wasn't watching.

I was now 60 pounds too heavy to wear the custom suits I'd been so proud of; I began to suspect I'd never wear them, that I'd just wasted two grand plus the time I'd put in with the tailor. I'd had the awareness to give myself a really nice nonfood reward, yet my addiction to food prevented me from enjoying it.

Without question, I'd slipped into one of my bad cycles. But, as disappointing as it was, there was something different about it this time, something positive and hopeful: I recognized what was happening relatively early, and I was able to arrest the process before spinning altogether out of control. In the past, my bad cycles tended to continue until I'd spiraled above my previous high weight and set a dispiriting new record. This time it didn't happen; for once I succeeded in putting on the brakes. This was far from perfection, but it was progress.

Partly this was a residual benefit of Pritikin. Rather than just obsessing about the numbers on the scale, I was paying more attention to how I *felt*—and the truth was I felt lousy. I was on the cusp of 50 years of age; maybe my body was just cutting me less slack. I'd always had aches in my back and knees and feet; now I also seemed to have a tendency toward strains and twinges in my arms and shoulders. At times I wondered if I was beginning to fall apart.

This didn't only worry me, it also made me angry. One of the important things I'd learned was that I didn't have to feel this bad. Maybe I didn't have a choice about being fat. I did have a choice about being a relatively healthy and active fat person, as opposed to a completely un-healthy, sedentary one. I finally got motivated to return to choosing better.

It was March 2, 1989, when I got back on the wagon. I weighed 288—nothing to be thrilled about, but more than 40 pounds shy of my 1984 peak. This time I decided to try a weight-loss regimen known as a protein-sparing fast.

Under the care of a well-regarded Washington in-ternist, I launched into an 800-calories-per-day diet that included almost nothing in the way of fats or carbohy-drates. My "food" consisted of three or four packets of a protein preparation that I mixed with fat-free milk or nonfat yogurt; the only other things I took in were calorie-free bouillon, various vitamin supplements, and large quantities of water. This was about as radical a diet as one could follow outside of a hospital and, not sur-prisingly, the weight came flying off. By late May, I'd lost 62 pounds and was down to 226.

But this experience was about more than simply shed-ding pounds: it was an important part of my ongoing ed-ucation about managing my fatness, and, at least indirectly, it started me on the road toward psychotherapy.

Aside from the diet itself and regular visits with the doctor, the protein-sparing program called for exercise and also for group classes and discussions on nutrition and life change. I went to the nutrition seminars but found myself avoiding the "change" groups. Why? Partly, I was uncomfortable with the language that tended to be used in that kind of setting. As a lawyer and a political guy, I was a rationalist; I mistrusted things that sounded soft and touchy-feely. Nor was I in-clined to bare my soul and share my deepest feelings with a bunch of strangers. And, to tell the truth, I didn't think I'd be all that interested in what the other group members had to say.

Besides, why worry about change when things were going well—while I was still losing weight? Through the spring I continued dropping pounds. At the end of 16 weeks—the maximum time one could stay on the diet—I was down to 217.

At that weight, I could finally have worn my beautiful custom suits. But I didn't get around to it soon enough. Within 2 weeks—*2 weeks!*—I'd started gaining again. As before, the process began slowly but took on an inexorable momentum.

By early August I'd gained 5 pounds. Then there was an upheaval in my professional life; a very positive development but stressful nonetheless. A friend of mine—a well-known Republican named Ken Duberstein—asked me if I would like to join him in launching a bipartisan government affairs consulting firm. As politics remained my passion, and as working in the legislative arena had become the dominant part of my legal practice, it didn't take me long to say yes. I resigned from the law firm of which I was a partner and gave up lawyering altogether.

Again, this was a refreshing change and a wonderful opportunity, but, inevitably, there was a certain amount of tension that went with both the logistics and the emotions of so major a transition. True to my old habits, I dealt with the stress by overeating. By Thanksgiving I'd put back 28 pounds and felt myself getting sucked into the grip of yet another upward spiral.

I was getting awfully tired of this. I mean literally tired: worn down, weary, drained by these seemingly endless alternations between hope and disappointment, between the belief that I was making progress and the fear that I was still mired in the same patterns that had plagued me since childhood. How many more times could I get excited about a weight-loss program that purported to be new, different, "scientific," the final answer? How many more times could I work my way back to any sort of physical conditioning after letting myself get sluggish and ill? How many more regressions could I go through before I simply gave up?

Something pretty basic was finally getting through to me: anyone could shed pounds on a radical diet for a finite length of time. That was the easy part. The hard part was life.

The challenge was living in such a way that the extreme ups and downs would cease or at least moderate. The real task lay in overcoming my compulsions and, if that proved to be impossible, at least managing them and understanding them better so that I had a chance of making peace. Health, happiness, and peace of mind were the really important goals, and those things were way beyond the reach of dieting alone. I was ready to try the change group.

I started attending weekly sessions, though that's about all I did—attend. I didn't really participate. I hardly spoke; I was seldom if ever moved to "share." When others talked, I nodded politely and mechanically to mask my lack of interest. I was not the least bit drawn to the psychologist who led the meetings.

Was that group a bad fit for me, or was it just my own continuing resistance? The only way to find out was to try a different group with a different leader. It so happened that Carol was participating in the same program at the time. Like me, she was still grappling with a lifelong tendency to put too much emphasis on food; like me, she was still looking for ways to stick with a healthy eating regimen. Unlike me, however, Carol seemed quite comfortable sharing her feelings in a group setting.

Her group was led by a psychologist named Bill, and she had a hunch that I would like him. Carol admired Bill's knack for combining sensitivity with a rigorous, no-nonsense approach to research data; she understood that I'd be more comfortable with a fact-based clinician than with someone dispensing feel-good generalities. Since husbands and wives could not attend the same sessions, Carol generously switched out of her group so I could give that one a try.

It turned out that I did like Bill, but I was still a bad camper in the group, silent and detached. What can I say? Group therapy is not for everyone, and it didn't seem to be for me. Uncomfortable and somewhat guilty, I once again stopped going altogether.

Then, in March of 1990, I came up with a different plan. I called Bill and asked if I could become an individual client. I started seeing him weekly; it was a relationship that would last nine years.

Here's an irony: After all my resistance and my several false starts, I really wish I'd begun my therapy decades sooner.

CHAPTER 12

GOING DEEP

Let me say from the start that I do not believe that psychotherapy can "cure" fatness. Then again, it is not my belief that fatness can be cured. You can't psychologize it away, any more than you can fix it once and for all with a new fad diet or a magic pill. My view, as I've argued, is that fatness is a chronic disease, a situation to be managed.

After 9 years of often hard and sometimes emotionally wrenching work, I cannot say with certainty that therapy has helped me lose one extra pound. I like to think that the awareness gained from therapy has helped me maintain my most recent weight loss, though I can't even be sure of that. Still, I feel that my therapy was a profoundly worthwhile experience. I would recommend psychotherapy to any fat person who can spare the time and money to pursue it; in fact, I'd recommend starting way earlier in life than I did and seeing one's therapist more often than the once a week that I was able to slot in.

Why do I feel that therapy was so valuable? I reckon its worth not in pounds but in knowledge. It comes down, finally, to the question of acceptance.

Being fat is more than just a physical fact. It is also a state of mind and a way of being in the world. Being fat defines us and marks us as different. Being different, in turn, inclines a person to imagine that there must be something *wrong* with him. Before my therapy, I bore a secret guilt. Why was I fat, when most people around me were not? Why didn't I eat like other people? Why couldn't I stop? Did I have some awful flaw? Was I goofy? Was I weird?

Therapy helped me understand many things about myself, my behavior, and my fatness—including some of the reasons I grew fat in the first place. I say "some" of the reasons because I believe that fatness is a complicated thing with multiple causes—brain chemistry, metabolism, probably heredity, not to mention environment and life experience—and no one discipline seems able to address them all.

But, in the course of talking to my therapist, I was able to air out many thoughts and often painful memories that bore connection to my weight. Some of these recollections were readily accessible and needed only a forum that allowed me to examine them in a systematic way. Other memories had been deeply buried and took years of work before I could finally bring them to light. I recalled, for example, certain humiliating episodes from childhood—incidents that had made me feel bad about my body and seemed unique and shameful. The difficulty of unearthing those secrets was equaled only by my relief in learning that my childhood embarrassments, and my reaction to them, were not so uncommon after all. Lots of kids experience physical humiliations that stay with them for decades or forever.

Therapy also provided fresh perspectives on a number of eating-related subjects—subjects that laypeople and even many regular physicians don't quite seem to understand.

Consider the issue of food and control. When I was bingeing or just eating unhealthily, the common perspective was that I was out of control. Viewed through the lens of psychotherapy, however, my insistence on eating whatever I wanted was a way of staying *in* control.

I asserted my independence and my personal sovereignty through food; no one else could tell me what to eat or when to stop. It's like that old Fats Waller lyric: "If I should eat two turkey dinners/Then say that it's just beginners/Ain't nobody's business if I do!"

This behavior, of course, was not in my own best interests, but that's a slightly different matter. The questions raised in therapy went further toward root causes: Why did I feel the need to prove to myself that I was in control? Why did I choose food as the way to do it? Why did I have to go to such extremes with it?

Over the years of my therapy, on the strength of a thousand tiny breakthroughs not infrequently glimpsed through tears, my fatness became easier to accept because it had begun to *make sense*. I was learning that the things I felt weren't crazy, and they didn't come from nowhere; I was a human being who'd been shaped—literally—by certain incidents and circumstances and by the responses that emerged from them.

In psychological terms, it was reasonable that I'd insulated myself with fatness. There was some logic to the powers I ascribed to food. These and other insights did not relieve me of responsibility for the choices I made, but they put those choices in a more complete and human context—a context in which people recognized them-selves as complex and vulnerable and less than perfect; where hard-edged notions like willpower and discipline just didn't have much meaning. I came to understand that I was dealing with not only my own weight but the weight of many things that had happened in my life.

In terms of my own chances for contentment, I believe the understandings I gained through therapy were ex-tremely important. But the progress I was making toward acceptance was a largely separate thing from my day-to day-struggles with the scale. The scale told me that I was as fat as ever and as much in thrall to the forces that had made me fat.

In April 1990, a month or so after I'd begun therapy, my weight was back up to 265. I decided to repeat the protein-sparing fast, but I found that I simply couldn't do it. I couldn't face those protein packets, that fat-free bouillon, that level of regimentation. I waited five days, took some deep breaths, and tried again; no go. Six weeks later and seven pounds heavier, I gave it another shot and was stymied once more.

It was the damnedest sensation, but I'm guessing that many fat people know what it's like. You're ready to start a diet; you want to start; in some way you're even *looking forward* to starting; but you don't start. Or you diet for one day . . . or part of a day . . . or a single meal . . . and then it's over. Does this mean you're in control or out of control? Frankly, it remains fairly mysterious to me.

Finally, in September, I managed to get myself back on the protein-sparing program. I lost 18 pounds in the first month, then, true to past experience, the diet just stopped working as well as it had the first time I'd tried it. Was it my body saying, *Wait a second, I've seen this trick before?* Was it my mind planting the negative suggestion, *I know perfectly well this isn't the ultimate solution?*

Whatever it was, the diet ended and the weight promptly came back. As of January 1991—nearly two years after I'd embraced the protein-sparing fast as my newest, brightest hope for a sustainable weight loss—I weighed 287. I'd had a net loss of exactly one pound.

My disappointment contributed to another problem as well: my commitment to exercise was trailing off. We all know the old saying, "When the going gets tough, the tough get going." If my experience is at all typical, I'd have to acknowledge that, when the going gets tough, the fat tend to *stop* going. Again, there is both a physical and a psychological reason for this. On the physical side, exercise gets to be sheer drudgery when you've gained a lot of

weight; everything hurts, nothing is fun. On the psychological side, one has to shout down a small, subversive
voice that says, *Why bother?* Clearly, these difficulties are
not unique to fat people; plenty of thin people slack off
when it comes to exercise. Still, fatness exacerbates the
problem. The joint pains that often go with carrying excess weight make even simple things like climbing stairs
a torment. Big bellies can literally block the way to certain abdominal exercises. It takes an act not only of will
but of blind faith to remember that exercise will in fact
improve your life and how you feel about yourself.

By that spring, I'd been in psychotherapy for over a
year—and I was still hiding food from Carol. I still hadn't
figured out why I needed to play that little game. I had no
problem eating as much as I wanted in front of anybody
else; friends, colleagues, and business associates had all
seen me eat prodigiously, unwisely, and without apology.
Why did I keep hiding food at home? The persistence of
this behavior made me feel that, when it came to food, I
still didn't understand what I was doing; I only knew that,
compulsively, I had to do it.

Like a squirrel, I seemed to have an instinct for
stashing away supplies of nuts. This would have been
okay if I'd been able to eat just a few at a time, but I

couldn't. When the impulse hit, I'd eat the whole bag of megacaloric cashews and Brazils. Once, when Carol was out of the apartment, I smuggled in an eight-pack of Hebrew National hot dogs. I cooked four in the microwave and wolfed them down. The dilemma was what to do with the others. I should have put them down the garbage disposal, but I didn't; I just put them, neatly wrapped, into the trash. An hour later they were in the microwave as well.

In relating these disappointments and ongoing frustrations, it is not my purpose to be discouraging. I relate them for two reasons. First, I've lived these setbacks—and survived them—and I'm determined to be honest about them. Second, I believe there is value in acknowledging that, in the struggle with fatness, as well as with the physical and emotional issues that fatness raises, there are no shortcuts and nothing comes easy. That's just how it is. If someone offers you a quick and painless fix, he's kidding you—or, more likely, trying to sell you something.

You don't wake up one morning to discover that you've defeated fatness—that you've gotten over it, as if it were a cold. Sure, there are certain people who get fat, then get thin, and for them the issue is resolved. But in general it doesn't work that way.

From day to day and year to year, what you *can* do is to alter your relationship with fatness so it loses the power to make you unhappy. Whatever the scale reads, there is value in trying to understand—so that understanding gradually replaces guilt, so that torment finally gives way to acceptance. That's a more realistic goal than magically becoming thin—and if you can accomplish it, it's victory enough.

Progress is where you find it. During the 1992 presidential campaign, for the first time ever at such a frenzied season, I didn't gain much weight.

Maybe this was because I already weighed 284 as the campaign was beginning. Maybe it was because I sensed we were finally going to win one! But there's another possibility as well. I like to think that maybe my awareness and understanding had grown to the point where a stressful situation didn't inevitably and automatically lead to a big weight gain. And if I could break out of that long-established pattern, maybe I could begin to free myself from others as well.

In any case, as that autumn went along I began spending weekends, then long weekends, then several weeks straight down in Little Rock, Arkansas, working for Bill Clinton. It was an exhausting but gratifying time.

Having been on the losing end of the last three presidential campaigns, it was great to be around a fresh young staff that was hopeful and undaunted.

When Clinton was elected I started receiving the usual invitations to appear on TV to talk about the new administration. As on certain earlier occasions, I turned them all down. This, I suppose, was an example of a situation in which I hadn't made much progress. I was still self-conscious and embarrassed about how fat I was; my ongoing therapy had not made me comfortable being outed on national television. I'd grown a beard, mainly to hide a double chin. Not that I really thought I was fooling anyone. The fact that I was hiding an extra chin was probably about as obvious as the chin itself would have been without the beard. Still, I was doing what I could to protect my little bit of vanity and make myself presentable in the eyes of the unfat world.

In other aspects of my life, too, this choppy, two-steps-forward, one-step-back sort of progress seemed to be the norm. For example, even as I gained more knowledge about the chronic nature and the vast complexity of fatness, some part of me still yearned for simple solutions—some magic formula that would suddenly change everything.

In early 1993, I began seeing a nutritionist—a woman with an excellent reputation who had helped many people move toward better and healthier eating habits. She was a good listener and treated her clients as individuals, designing custom programs rather than pushing a one-size-fits-all diet. I had eight visits with her, and when I didn't see dramatic results, I stopped going. Why?

The problem was not with the nutritionist; it was my expectations that were out of whack. I'd been fat for 50 years; was she supposed to be able to set me on a straight and narrow path toward thinness in two or three months? Could any practitioner or any program be reasonably expected to do that? Stepping back, it seems clear that the answer is no.

But stepping back is precisely the hard part. When a fat person so desperately wants to be thinner, it's difficult to see beyond that yearning and get an accurate sense of what constitutes a realistic objective and a sane means of achieving it.

To put it another way, part of making peace with one's fatness is learning to manage expectations. One has to recognize the difference between a worthwhile, attainable goal and an unrealistic fantasy that can only lead to more self-blame and more frustration. For better or worse, this does not seem to be a lesson that people learn all at once. I've chased my share of fantasies—more of them, I must admit, than seems quite rational—and I believe that's pretty typical. The good news is that, as I've gone along, I've gotten harder to fool—and less likely to fool myself.

Let me give one more illustration of the halting but real progress by which I believe that I've been coming to understand, accept, and to some degree control my fatness.

As I've discussed, I've been sneaking food and hiding food ever since I was a child. The ways and means of my doing this have varied over the years, but the behavior itself has been a constant: a compulsion.

In 1993, Carol and I, needing more space and a guest room, bought a second apartment a few doors down the hall from the one that we lived in. The main room of this apartment became my home office. We called it the Growlery—a reference to the Dickens novel *Bleak House*, in which the central character has a "growlery" he can slip off to when he needs to brood. I did a fair bit of brooding as well as working in my own personal growlery, and I enjoyed having a retreat right in my own backyard.

The second apartment had its own small kitchen, a place that Carol seldom visited. I could stash extra food right there in the cupboards or the little fridge and probably get away with it. Yet I continued hiding goodies—cookies, saltines, egg-salad sandwiches—in much more secret places. I hid food in my wastebasket; behind my computer; on the floor beneath my printer. I didn't need to do this to avoid detection; it seems hiding food was a game I didn't know how to stop playing.

But around this time I made a remarkable discovery, a kind of personal breakthrough. I realized that I didn't really enjoy my furtive eating.

Eating furtively had been one of the central facts of my life. Since it seemed I had to do it, it really didn't matter how I felt about it, whether or not I enjoyed it. I had to do it, period.

Now, finally, I had achieved some distance; I could make a conscious judgment. I could acknowledge that eating lukewarm things from greasy wrapping paper wasn't very elegant or pleasing. More important, I'd begun to recognize that food alone—without the amenities and social rituals that accompanied it in "normal" situations—was not all-sufficient or completely satisfying. I was beginning to see that food was part of something wonderful—namely, life—but it wasn't life itself.

Did this mean that I suddenly stopped hiding food or eating on the sly? No, that would be too easy and too neat. I hide food to this day. But furtive eating is far less important to me than it used to be, and, more important, my attitude about it has evolved. I no longer see it as a dark and shameful secret, evidence of my being a weird or weak person; I regard it as an eccentricity, odd but certainly not an evil quirk. I have largely left behind my guilt about it; I am more likely to regard my own behavior with a shrug and a wink. I have learned that if I cut myself a little slack—if I don't berate myself for sneaking food now and then—I'm less likely to let the sneaking get excessive.

To put it another way, I control my furtive eating by accepting it. And, as I'll explain, I believe that this idea of control through acceptance also pertains to other aspects of managing one's fatness, of living well while living large.

CHAPTER 13

FITNESS 101

I have heard a rumor that there are people in the world who really love to exercise. People who are never happier than when pulling on their sneakers and heading out for a run or bounding off to the gym or tennis club. People who take great joy in throwing a ball or catching one; people who look natural with sweaty towels bunched around their necks. I admire these people and wish them well.

My own relationship with exercise has been far more problematic and strewn with small disasters. When I was a boy, these misadventures took the form of a baseball bat to the teeth or a hockey puck to the chin; as an adult, my mishaps have included pulled muscles and torn cartilage. But if I've occasionally hurt myself while working out, I've learned by now that I've hurt myself more by *not* working out.

When it comes to exercise, I have been, for most of my life, reluctant and inconsistent. Beginning with my experience at Pritikin, there have been periods when I've exercised regularly, with heartening, even dramatic, results. But those episodes have tended to be pegged to some particular weight-loss crusade; as my enthusiasm for a given eating regimen fell away, so did my commitment to exercise. Earlier in these pages, I alluded to the Greek root of our word *diet*. The original meaning, you'll recall, was simply "way of life." Well, that precisely sums up what was lacking in my attitude toward exercise. I approached it as an aspect of "dieting" in the modern sense of the word, but I had failed to really make it part of my life's routine.

In the early 1990s, when I was past the age of 50, that finally began to change. I had learned a couple things that really struck me, that constituted a sort of carrot-and-stick incentive to get fitter.

The carrot had to do with mortality rates, which decrease in men as they become more fit. But here's what really got my attention: Research showed that as fat men got fitter, their mortality rates became no greater than those of leaner men who were fit. In other words, if one stayed fit, one could hope to have a normal life expectancy in spite of being fat. This reinforced my growing awareness that it wasn't only pounds that mattered but health as well.

The stick had to do with something I'd read about people who ended up in nursing homes. In a significant percentage of cases, people needed nursing homes, not necessarily because they were sick or senile, but because they lacked the strength, mobility, and flexibility to perform daily tasks without assistance—basic things like getting dressed, or getting into or out of a bathtub, or rising from a commode. Since problems with mobility are exacerbated by fatness, this was a clear wake-up call to make sure I could keep my body moving.

There was no lightning-bolt moment when my attitude toward exercise suddenly changed, but I date my "new" approach to fitness as of 1991 and a two-week residency program I attended at the Canyon Ranch spa outside of Tucson. There, at the Life Enhancement Center—a sort of spa-within-a-spa dedicated to weight loss and smoking cessation—I followed a workout regimen that featured lots of walking and resistance training; it was a well-thought-out program tailored to my needs and abilities at the time. There were also meetings and lectures that tended to stress a single, simple theme: that the work we were doing there was not about suffering or deprivation; it was about making our lives better.

Pretty basic. And I think it was finally getting through to me. I went home to D.C., kept on exercising, kept on feeling pretty good, kept on losing weight. For a while.

My progress once again was not linear or constant. After several months I began to fall away from my routine. The good news was: I noticed. I noticed that I had less energy. I noticed that I felt less flexible and less strong. I noticed, even, that I was more likely to feel grumpy. To my own amazement, and for the first time in my life, I noticed that I was *missing* exercise. Was it possible? Maybe fitness was finally becoming part of my way of life.

One day in the spring of 1992, I was walking down a street near my office and saw a sign for a gym called One to One. I was intrigued . . . but ambivalent. Most of my more serious exercising had been done either at either the cozy, homey YMCA or in specialized residential settings, where there were other fat people around, as well as trainers who understood fat bodies. I had generally been put off—and frankly, intimidated—by private gyms. They tended to be filled with lean people in spandex who strutted around with a physical confidence that only added to my self-consciousness. In the private gyms I'd seen, there were very few people who were shaped like me.

Still, I had a few minutes to spare and nothing to lose, so I went in. Right from the start, there were several things I liked about the facility. First, it was small; it seemed manageable, not frenetic and overwhelming like other gyms I'd seen. A maximum of seven people worked out at a time, each with his or her own trainer; I liked this, as well, because I still had much to learn about exercise techniques, plus a commitment to a trainer would reinforce my discipline about showing up. Sessions were 45 minutes long, which seemed reasonable and would fit into my schedule. Best of all, both clients and trainers were dressed in simple, loose-fitting clothes provided by the gym. (It turned out that they didn't have any of these standard-issue items in anything close to my size, but that was okay. At least I wasn't surrounded by people dressed in clothing that sparkled.) I signed up.

My first session was devoted to evaluating my physical condition and designing my program, and here I made the first of several mistakes I would commit along the way. I asked for sessions that consisted almost entirely of weight lifting and other forms of resistance training. This, of course, was a typical guy thing—to put too much emphasis on building strength and too little on flexibility and cardiovascular fitness. The manager urged me to dedicate more of my workout time to cardio; I assured her that I'd do cardio on my own. I had both a treadmill and a stationary bike at home, so what was the problem?

The problem, of course, was that at home there was always plenty to do other than walking the treadmill or riding the bike. At the gym, there was nothing to do except work out; I gradually saw the wisdom of doing my cardio there.

This first misstep aside, my new fitness regimen got off to a fine start, and even better, I found that I was sticking with it. When I was home in Washington, I generally worked out four mornings a week; when business took me away from home, I found that I was actually eager to get back to the gym. Maybe this was just guilt or compulsiveness, but I prefer to think I wanted to get back because I was happy with the results I was seeing. I felt stronger and enjoyed the feeling. My blood pressure and cholesterol were in an acceptable range, and I had the pleasure of knowing I was being good to myself. I must have discovered endorphins; after a vigorous workout, I felt physically energized and emotionally high.

But let me be clear about what my time in the gym was *not* doing for me. It was not—in the near term, at least—leading to stellar results in my effort to control my weight. In 1992, when I launched into my program, I weighed 268. At the end of 1994, after almost two years of pretty good adherence to my regimen and with several of my usual ups and downs along the way, I weighed 315.

My point is not to negate the value of the exercise. I believe the exercise was very valuable on its own terms. For one happy moment, let's forget the scale! Whatever the scale said, I knew that I was healthier and stronger, that there was a spring in my step, that the increase in my physical activity had improved my quality of life. Exercise was not making me a thin person, but it was making me better at being the person I happened to be.

In this, I think, an analogy can be drawn between my exercise program and my psychotherapy. Neither was a "cure" for fatness, yet both were powerful antidotes for the ways that fatness, if unexamined and unmanaged, can diminish a life. Both promoted well-being and peace of mind at any weight.

I am happy to report that even today, at the age of 66, I still try to put in four mornings a week at the gym; in fact, I've added the luxury of a massage and, most weeks, a fifth morning, devoted to a one-to-one yoga session. As of this writing, according to records kept by the gym, I have exercised there on more than 1,950 occasions. I like knowing that my appearances are being written down, that I'm getting credit for showing up. This is an incentive to keep going back.

Do I ever play hooky or just drag myself halfheartedly through a workout? Of course; everybody does, and it's nothing to be ashamed of or to get discouraged about. Meanwhile, I have continued to learn things about exercise, about my own body, about my capabilities as well as my limits. I have also continued to make my share of mistakes.

Back in the mid-1990s, when I was more gung-ho than knowledgeable about the new things I was doing, I spent a lot of time feeling very beat up after exercise. Feet, knees, lower back, shoulders—everything seemed to hurt, and the pain was bringing me close to quitting. It turned out I was overtraining.

Overtraining? Me? Yes, the truth was I was simply trying to do too much. Looking back, I think there were two reasons for this. First, it was that compulsive thing again. Second, I was trying too hard to do what I imagined my trainer wanted me to do, to measure up to some real or imagined set of expectations that weren't right for *me*.

One day while I was on the StairMaster, I told the senior trainer that I was seriously considering giving up because I'd been experiencing too much postexercise discomfort for too long. He looked at me as if I had two heads and asked why I hadn't said something sooner. A very good question! The answer, I suppose, was that I hadn't realized that I could—and should—assert some control over my own program. The trainers may have been the experts, but no one except me could know what it was like to live inside my body.

That was my last session with the StairMaster and the VersaClimber; I began spending more time on the treadmill, the bicycle, and the rower. I lightened up on weights, did more for flexibility—and felt a whole lot better. As in so many other aspects of my life, I was learning as I went along.

Because I've come to feel that regular exercise is extremely important for overall well-being, and because I know firsthand of the particular difficulties and discouragements that fat people face when trying to get fit, I want to take a little time to offer some specific, commonsense advice.

Let's first address a fundamental question: Given that exercise alone is not a weight-loss panacea or guarantee, why should fat people bother working out at all?

The simplest answer is that, if my personal experience is any indication, you'll feel better, happier, and more physically confident if you do. Working out offers a wide range of benefits that are independent of the question of weight. Among them:

- Regular exercise helps lower blood pressure and increase the level of "good" cholesterol.
- Working out can help relieve mild to moderate depression and anxiety.
- Regular exercisers tend to sleep better. They fall asleep faster, sleep longer, and are awake less during the night.
- Exercise promotes strength and flexibility that make performing everyday tasks easier and more comfortable and will help keep you mobile to an older age.

The key concept here—a profound, far-reaching one—is *functionality*. Regular exercise allows you to do more—climbing stairs, gardening, playing with the grandkids or the dog, whatever. Doing more, in turn, leads to continuing functionality, allowing you to remain independent longer and maintain the dignity and self-respect that go with independence. Also, while I caution that exercise alone should not be regarded as a miracle cure for fatness, I strongly believe that working out can and should be part of any ongoing and sustainable weight-control campaign.

The sad truth is that it takes a hell of a lot of exercise to burn off any appreciable amount of fat; fat, after all, is a very concentrated form of caloric energy. That said, exercise is a very efficient way to burn calories—and losing weight comes down, finally, to burning more calories than you take in. But there is also a benefit that continues long after you leave the gym. Exercise builds muscle, and muscle is more metabolically active than fat is. When you put on muscle, you effectively speed up your metabolism, and you burn more calories even when at rest. This is why, in my view, exercise is very important in terms of *maintaining* weight loss.

For all these clear benefits, however, there are also serious hurdles and disincentives facing fat people who want to get fitter.

- Fat people who have not been working out tend to have poor stamina and are easily winded and fatigued. Even light exercise is daunting at the start; it seems tough to accomplish much if one tires so quickly.

- In many if not most commercial gyms, fat people are seriously under-represented. Being surrounded by lean people in formfitting clothes can be alienating and intimidating.
- Of the many fitness books and videos available, few take the special needs of fat people into account. Trying to "get with a program" that was designed for a very different body type can quickly become discouraging.
- There are a lot of irresponsible or bogus claims out there that also breed discouragement. Nothing is likelier to produce a fitness dropout than the disappointment that comes from chasing a phantom goal.

And then there's the simple fact that, until exercise really becomes a part of your life, it just seems easier not to do it. Why buy sneakers? Why get sweaty? It's so much easier to sit on the couch—and get fatter, and weaker, and less flexible, and less healthy.

How, then, can a fat person get past the inertia, shyness, and fear to get started on a realistic and sustainable fitness program? Here are some things that will help.

Make a plan. This doesn't have to be detailed or precise, just a general road map of what you hope to accomplish. Write it down—things seem clearer and more real that way. Consider your exercise history. What sort of activities have you done in the past? What have you enjoyed? What did you find of value? What hurt or was otherwise unpleasant? If you've tried and quit a fitness program before, why did you give up? Try to clarify your thoughts so you'll have a better chance of truly starting fresh.

An important aspect of your plan should be the question of frequency. How often will you work out? How much time are you willing to devote?

In its recently revised diet guidelines, the federal government recommends a minimum of 30 minutes of exercise *every day* for maintaining general health, and as much as 90 minutes a day of physical activity if you are trying to lose weight. Of course, this "physical activity" is pretty loosely defined, including things like housework (which men tend not to do) and yard work (which I, for one, have always avoided). In terms of actual workouts, my view is that three one-hour sessions a week is a reasonable minimum for seeing meaningful results; four or five would be better.

However often you work out, don't be casual about how you fit exercise into your schedule. You are making an important commitment. Honor that commitment by treating your workouts as a serious appointment, as you would a meeting at work or a social event.

Consult your doctor. The first requirement of any exercise program is that it be safe—and while virtually everyone can exercise at some level of strenuousness, individual limitations need to be taken into account. As fat people tend to have a higher than average incidence of health issues like hypertension, heart disease, and orthopedic problems, these things need to be factored in. Typically, for instance, people are advised to exercise at 80 to 85 percent of peak cardiovascular capacity; does that figure make sense for *you*? Carrying excess weight is tough on joints, especially hips, knees, and ankles; are your joints so compromised that you're better off doing your exercise in a pool?

Consider an exercise evaluation. This is not absolutely necessary—availability and expense may be issues—but it is helpful to work with a professional to get an accurate sense of your strength, flexibility, and endurance. Whether or not you continue working with a trainer, this will get your program established in a sound and healthy way.

Location, location, location. This is crucial. If you are not comfortable where you work out, the place itself becomes an excuse to quit. Conversely, if you're happy with your spot, it will pull you back for more.

Some people prefer to exercise at home; it's private, comfortable, and convenient. But will you have the discipline to stick with a home program? I found that I did not. Before you invest in expensive exercise equipment, ask yourself if you honestly believe you'll use it.

Gyms present a different set of issues. Is your gym convenient to where you live or work? Will the time it takes to get there, the traffic, or the parking prove a disincentive? How about the little things—the lighting, the music? Is the atmosphere friendly? Is it snobby?

By all means, try to find a gym where you will be comfortable as a fat person; i.e., not feel that you have wandered onto the set of *Baywatch* or are backstage at the Mr. Universe contest. In general, I have found that exercise professionals as well as the vast majority of unfat people are understanding and supportive of fat people's efforts to get fit. There will always be a few who let their biases show.

Respect your own preferences. You're a grown-up— you don't have to do things you don't want to do. When it comes to exercise, there are almost always multiple ways to achieve a particular objective. Your chances of

sticking with a program are much better if you emphasize activities you find congenial.

Consider strength training. If you like the feel of free
weights, go ahead and use them. You *don't* like free
weights? Try the Cybex or Nautilus machines. You find
machines too complicated? No problem. Use those
simple color-coded resistance bands. Any of the above
will make you stronger.

Similarly with flexibility: Can't stand old-fashioned
calisthenics? Try yoga. Yoga has too much mumbo jumbo
for you? Okay, try Pilates or just rolling on a stability ball.
Follow a CD or videotape. There are hundreds of them,
though few have been designed specifically for fat people;
there's no shame in modifying some of the moves. Listen
to your body. Pain is its way of telling you to stop

Again, in regard to aerobics: Walking the treadmill
bores you to tears? Try a stationary bike or rowing ma-
chine with variable programs. Or use one of fat people's
relatively few athletic advantages—buoyancy—and take
up swimming.

Also, keep in mind that what you *don't* do is an important part of a good program. For instance, very fat
people probably shouldn't run or jog; it puts too much
stress on knees and ankles. Jogging on pavement is a def-

inite no-no; but in my view any sort of running is probably a foolish idea for people whose joints are carrying a lot of extra weight.

Bottom line: Don't do things that hurt. Don't do things you hate.

My own workout has evolved over the years, but here are the essentials. I do 15 minutes on the treadmill, getting the heart rate up to 75 or 80 percent of maximum and also warming up the muscles. Then I do 45 minutes of what's called "circuit training." The idea is to alternate strength-building exercise with enough aerobics to keep the heart rate up. Some parts of my workout have been customized to accommodate my weight. For example, I do push-ups against a bar rather than going all the way to the floor. Again, the point is to find a realistic program that works for the body you have.

After almost 2,000 sessions at my gym, can I tell you in all honesty that I *enjoy* my workouts? Not really. I do them because I see a benefit, because I know they're good for me. Without question, there's a certain satisfaction, and even pleasure, in having worked out. But loving it as I'm actually doing it? That might be asking a little too much.

Have a Plan B. It's great to have a regular exercise routine, but don't become so dependent on a particular location or set of equipment that you feel you can't work out without it. If you're like most people, your schedule will sometimes be disrupted by business travel or vacation. So be open to kinds of exercise that can be done almost anywhere—floor stretching, strength work with resistance bands, and so forth.

Of particular value, but too easily overlooked, is walking. Walking is terrific exercise and particularly well suited to fat people; walking fast, whether outdoors or on a treadmill, has all the aerobic benefits of running, with few of the orthopedic drawbacks. It's also a form of exercise in which progress can be easily measured. Back when I first went to Pritikin, I could barely walk two blocks; in later years I found it possible to go 15 miles, with just a short rest at the halfway point. That's gratifying.

Moreover, walking is the ultimate in portability. All you need are your feet and a comfortable pair of shoes or sneakers. There is no more interesting way to get to know a new city than by strolling through its streets. At home, try multiple routes, and drive them by car to compare distances. It's gratifying to see how far you've gone.

Walking can be either a central aspect of your program or a Plan B when your program is disrupted. Either way, it belongs in your repertoire.

Be realistic. Let's face it—most of us who incline to be extremely fat are never going to have what most would call a perfect body. We're not likely to go from being couch potatoes to triathletes. But that's not the point of exercise. The point of exercise is to make us better at being who we are. The aim is to become fitter and healthier by our own standards, not by standards imposed by other people.

By all means, set goals—but make sure those goals are reasonable and attainable. Consider, for example, the question of duration.

A solid exercise program generally demands a minimum of 30 minutes of strenuous activity. At the start, you might not have the stamina to do nearly that much. If you can do only five minutes on the treadmill, fine— that's five minutes more than nothing. Soon you'll be doing ten. If you can steal ten minutes three times a day, that's almost as beneficial as working out for half an hour at a clip. And eventually you *will* be able to do that much, or more. At this point, my program, including warm-up and cool-down, lasts about an hour. I could not have done nearly that much at the start.

My progress was gradual; yours will be too. Don't expect sudden breakthroughs or radical transformations because that isn't how it works. The real victory lies in incremental progress; that progress becomes its own reward. There's no incentive quite so reliable as seeing actual improvement.

Be gentle with yourself. I mean this both physically and emotionally. Let's start with the physical part.

One of the benefits of exercise is that it puts us in closer touch with our bodies. I've spoken earlier about the use of fat as an insulator from life. It occurs to me that fatness can even insulate us from ourselves. It is easy to forget that, beneath our layer of fat, there are muscles and bones and sinews—and those things are *us*. Exercise reminds us that this is so. With that increased awareness, we can take greater pleasure in our strength, in our movement. We can also better discern the difference between a healthy, well-earned fatigue and an injury. It's important to know how hard to push yourself, when to rest, and when to seek medical care for something that doesn't feel right.

On the emotional side, being gentle with yourself basically comes down to this: don't expect or demand perfection. No one shows up for each and every scheduled workout. No one has the same strength or energy every day. Some days you just won't feel like exercising. That's okay. Don't feel guilty about missing sessions now and then; the guilt itself can too easily become an excuse for giving up.

Understand that your progress will not be perfectly smooth or steady. Advances often lead to plateaus, bewildering roadblocks that make it seem that further improvement will never come. Relax. Everybody hits plateaus. And there is always further progress once you work your way past them.

At some point, you may notice that a surprising—even amazing—change has taken place: It's now easier to exercise than not to! Working out has become, if not an actual pleasure, then at least a habit, occupying a secure and stable place in your routine. When that happens, exercise is no longer a penance or one more painful aspect of dieting; it has become a part of your own *diaita*.

CHAPTER 14

WHEN THE FAT HITS THE FAN

Addicts—whether their problem is tobacco or alcohol or drugs—tend to imagine that, faced with a true crisis or a real threat to their well-being, they would be able to walk away from their addiction at any time. At certain stages of my life, I seem to have been prey to the same illusion. I'd always told myself that if my fatness ever led to real health problems—not just aching knees and feet but something truly serious—then *of course* I'd be able to get my eating under control, take off weight, and keep it off.

In 1995 I was forced to put that assumption to the test.

During my annual physical, by way of a routine urine sample, my doctor spotted signs of a possible kidney problem. The next step was to do a 24-hour urine collection, followed by a sonogram of my kidneys. Right from the start, it became clear that my fatness was making everything, even the diagnostic process, more complicated and more difficult. The doctor who administered the sonogram could neither detect nor rule out kidney stones; my excess fat made it impossible to get a sufficiently clear image.

I was told that I would need to see a nephrologist and probably have a biopsy. Specialists, biopsies—it was starting to get scary. Did this affect my behavior, so far as my overeating was concerned? Let me answer that by reporting one of my regular routines from around this time.

I worked out almost every Saturday morning. Near my gym, unfortunately, there was a bagel place. After my exercise session, I'd stop in there and give my usual order: two bagels, one with kosher salami, the other sliced but plain. I'd take the treat back to my home or office, carefully divide the salami between the two bagels, and polish them both off. Thus, after a workout that burned perhaps 200 calories, I'd "reward" myself with a high-fat, high-carb, high-sodium, high-everything snack that contained a thousand calories or more. Did I know better? Of course. Did my knowledge determine my actions? Obviously not.

In any case, I went to see the nephrologist. He ordered

a blood test, noted that my blood pressure and cholesterol were elevated, and confirmed that a biopsy would be required. And here, once again, my size made things more complicated.

There are two kinds of biopsies: "closed" and "open." Open is the kind you don't want; it involves an invasive surgical procedure. A closed biopsy is done through a needle and is far simpler. But the needle has to be able to get through to the organ being tested. The more fat between the skin and the organ, the harder it is to do; at some point it becomes impossible.

I qualified for the closed biopsy, but just barely. Because of my fatness, the procedure was difficult and awkward, requiring an overnight hospital stay. It confirmed that I did, in fact, have a kidney problem—a condition called focal glomerulosclerosis and tubular interstitial nephritis. While not immediately life-threatening, the condition can, if it advances, lead eventually to renal failure. Renal failure means that you either become a dialysis patient, have a kidney transplant, or die.

The causes? These seem to be multiple. But it is generally believed that high blood pressure is an accelerator, and high cholesterol is most likely a factor as well. Some opinion holds that fatness itself is a contributing cause;

whether or not this is the case, fatness certainly correlates with the other possible factors. There is no known treatment, except to try to stop the disease from accelerating by lowering blood pressure and cholesterol. Losing weight, of course, would help with both those goals.

So there it was. I was 56 years old, and I finally had clear, compelling evidence that my fatness was threatening my health.

This was a somewhat different sort of problem from any I had faced before. When I was young and my fatness held me back from certain aspects of a "normal" social life, I found ways to compensate: I learned to create a different kind of social life. At college and in my profession, I learned how to minimize the negative effects of my size or even to turn it to an advantage. Through my psychotherapy, I was starting to learn how to make peace with the emotional aspects of my fatness.

In all these situations, my fatness was a given—an essential part of who I was and who I expected I would always be—and the challenge lay in finding ways to work around it. But how did one work around poor health? How did one compensate for being sick?

To my disappointment and genuine surprise, these new health concerns didn't seem to make it any easier for me to take off weight. At the time of my diagnosis, I tipped the scale at 277 pounds. During the next year or so, my weight wobbled in what, for me, was a pretty narrow range—10 pounds here, 20 pounds there. Then, in 1997, I started on yet another upward track. I began the year at 289 and ended it at 309.

Remember those gorgeous custom suits I'd splurged on, that I was so proud of, back in the mid-1980s? Nineteen ninety-seven was the year I finally gave them away, never having worn them.

Viewed from a certain perspective, my failure to lose weight in the face of my new health issues seems baffling, perverse, even infuriating. Was I trying to hurt myself? What more motivation did I need?

Looked at another way, however, it's really not surprising that I continued to struggle with my weight. As I've argued, I believe that my kind of chronic fatness is a disease. Why would we imagine that one disease would cure another? Would I mysteriously "get over" being fat because I now had kidney problems too? Or would my "new" disease just be added on to the difficulties I'd contended with my entire life?

From my point of view, it certainly seemed that I was getting to a stage when problems were starting to pile onto other problems. For many years, as I've mentioned, I'd had pain in my knees and ankles—a perhaps inevitable consequence of asking my joints to bear so much extra weight for so long. Around this time, my knees started to hurt so badly, particularly when climbing stairs, that my doctor sent me to a rheumatologist.

Another specialist! And another confirmation of a troubling diagnosis. After many x-rays and much manipulation, it became clear that I had osteoarthritis in my knees.

The good news was that there was a medication available that provided a significant measure of relief. The bad news was that it suddenly seemed that I was taking a hell of a lot of medications, all of them for actual or potential conditions connected to my weight. I took two different pills for blood pressure; one to lower my cholesterol; one for my arthritic knees; half an aspirin for my at-risk heart.

I was not yet 60, and, medically speaking, I was starting to resemble an old man. My medicine chest was cluttered with prescription bottles. Inevitably, my health concerns and physical limitations also had an impact on Carol; it was as if, in some odd way, I was tugging her along with me in the aging process. Shortly after I was put on Lipitor, so was she. My growing awareness that my knees were shot made Carol very cautious about *her* knees; she gave up tennis. She missed our long walks together; so did I.

In any case, my medical history was taking on the heft and subplots of a saga. I no longer had a doctor but a team of doctors. There was no denying it: my fatness was accelerating the normal aging process.

Throughout this book, I have tried to make a number of points in which I passionately believe:

That it is not the goal of life to be thin but to be happy and fulfilled; that fatness is no excuse for holding back from the richness and variety of living; that if a fat person is who you are, then accept it, make your peace with it, and hold on to the self-respect that you deserve no less than any other person.

At the same time, it would be irresponsible and just plain wrong to deny that being fat has consequences. Real, physical consequences. And, however well one deals with the social, professional, and emotional challenges of fatness, the physical hazards cannot be ignored or wished away.

The bottom line is that fatness is likely to be bad for

your health. I say "likely" because the health risks of obesity are a subject of enormous controversy, one in which the stakes are high. Drug companies, insurers, and even governments are in on the debate; in many studies, it is difficult to separate the science from the politics. Still, the preponderance of responsible opinion is that serious fatness will sooner or later make you sick. One study suggests that between 80 and 90 percent of fat people will develop health problems related to their fatness. Whatever the precise figures, the basic fact seems to be beyond argument. From the perspective of physical wellness, if you *can* lose weight, you *should* lose weight.

But, as I know as well as anyone, that is one very big *if.*

If I could lower my blood pressure by dropping 50 pounds and keeping it off, of course I would. *If* I could ease the strain on my arthritic knees by becoming substantially lighter, of course I would. But in the meantime, I've got a more immediate issue to face—an issue that confronts all of us who are chronically fat: how can I best see to my health *as I actually am*?

Exercise, as we've discussed, is part of the equation. So, for me, was psychotherapy. But there is also the nitty-gritty of facing up to the special risks that go with fatness, as well as figuring out how to deal responsibly and effectively with members of the medical profession.

Let me pass along some things I've learned and some advice I've gathered over many years of living with these issues.

Know the risks. It has been suggested that well over 100,000 deaths annually are caused by fatness. This, in my view, is one those attention-grabbing statistics that turn out, on closer inspection, to be rather meaningless. Except in a very small number of extreme cases, people don't die of being fat. (There's also the fact that thin people die too.) That said, plenty of people die of things that *correlate* with fatness. But diseases almost never have a single cause; there is no one-to-one correspondence between fatness and, say, heart attacks.

In other words, when it comes to the specific health risks of fatness, there are a lot of gray areas; and, human nature being what it is, where there are gray areas, people believe what they want to believe. Some people make the potentially fatal error of imagining that they are somehow exempt from the physically damaging effects of fatness. Others go to the opposite extreme and literally make themselves sick with worry. The challenge is to come up with a rational and honest assessment of what the health risks are for you.

Do certain diseases seem to run in your family? If so, then heredity is a risk factor in addition to your fatness. Have you kept up your cardiovascular fitness? Then you've probably reduced your risk of certain problems.

There are at least a couple of dozen diseases, known as comorbidities, that are more than casually associated with obesity. It's beyond our scope to consider them all, but let's look briefly at just a few that are either quite closely linked to weight or illustrate some of the not always obvious ways in which fatness connects with other problems.

Type 2 diabetes is a condition in which the body can not produce enough insulin to allow for proper cell metabolism. Seriously fat people are up to 40 times more likely to develop this disease than are lean people. Diabetes, in turn, can be a cause of further problems, including kidney failure and blindness.

High blood pressure, or hypertension, is another problem linked to fatness and can lead to a host of other maladies, including stroke. My own kidney problem is attributable, at least in part, to hypertension.

Colorectal cancer's correlation with fatness is not so readily apparent. It is probably a matter of diet; people who are substantially overweight are more likely to have a diet that is high in fat and low in fiber. These same factors also lead to a higher incidence in fat people of gall-bladder disease.

Now, everyone will die of something; becoming thin will not make you immortal. But, if you are fat, you are prey to certain special risks. Don't kid yourself about that; don't bury your head in the sand. Acknowledging those risks is the first step in trying to mitigate them.

Pick the right health-care people. It is a disappointing truth that doctors, nurses, and even nutritionists and psychotherapists are not immune to the same antifat biases that prevail among the general public. Study after study has confirmed this. In one survey of health professionals involved in the treatment of fatness, 87 percent of the respondents thought that fat people were "self-indulgent"; fully a third thought fat people lacked willpower. Another survey of physicians found that just shy of half did not consider counseling fat people about weight loss to be "professionally gratifying." Similarly, interviews with nurses have revealed that their emotional reactions to fat people include "guilt, disgust, embarrassment, hopelessness, and resentment."

This kind of prejudice is not likely to help a person. A doctor who makes you feel guilty or a nurse who shows disdain in touching you performs a disservice both to you and to the medical profession. Don't be afraid to leave a doctor who seems insensitive to your situation. Don't settle for grudging attention from a nurse who clearly would rather not be treating you.

Fortunately, there are plenty of health-care professionals who are above these biases—but you have to seek them out. I have generally been lucky in this regard. Not that I've been coddled or showered with unconditional love; that's not the point. The point is that I've met with realism. I've dealt with doctors and nurses who have regarded my fatness not as a character flaw or a moral failing but as a chronic disease, a preexisting condition that must be factored in.

Have my doctors advised me that losing weight would be a good idea? Of course they have; they'd be derelict in their duties if they didn't. Have they browbeaten me about it? No. Have they made me feel guilty when I haven't managed it? No—they have been wise enough to understand that guilt and shame can only be counterproductive.

Communicate. Many studies suggest that when a patient is unhappy with a doctor, the cause is less likely to be lack of faith in the physician's healing skills than problems in communication.

It is a sad truth that doctors don't always listen as well as they ought to. In this age of managed care and mounting economic pressures, most doctors see a lot of patients and are generally squeezed for time. That said, communication is a two-way street, and the patient also bears responsibility for making sure that all the necessary information is exchanged. As a patient, it's your job to:

- Convey whatever facts the doctor needs regarding your history and your current situation.
- Ask whatever questions you have pertaining to your condition, without fear of seeming uninformed or stupid.
- Make sure those questions are answered in a way that you can understand.
- Because face time with the doctor is generally at a premium, and because it's hard to think perfectly straight when you're a nervous patient in a doctor's office, write down notes to bring to an appointment. The more prepared you are, the more you'll get out of the consultation.

Coordinate. One physical problem tends to lead to another, and, unless you are extremely fortunate in your health, there will probably come a point where you have several doctors in your life. Over the last several years I have seen, in addition to my primary-care physician and my psychologist, a nephrologist, a urologist, a rheumatologist, a cardiologist, a gastroenterologist, a dermatologist, an orthopedist, a podiatrist, and a dentist. And I'm not in that bad shape!

The point is that different people will be treating various aspects of your total health, and, just as it your responsibility to communicate effectively with each individual caregiver, it is your job to coordinate what they know about you.

If a given doctor orders a test, make sure that all relevant physicians get the results. If a specialist finds a significant change in a particular condition, make sure you discuss this with your primary doctor. If the information is more technical than you can confidently convey, then make sure they talk to each other. Don't assume they do. Things have a way of falling through cracks; don't let your health be one of them.

Educate yourself. Medical language can be intimidating, but once you get past the mumbo jumbo, the basics of most diseases are well within the ability of laypeople to understand. If you are diagnosed with some adverse condition, do everything you can to learn about it.

This should start—but not end—with talking to your doctor. There is always reading to be done: informational brochures, books designed for general audiences, a mass of information available on the Internet. Aside from the specific, practical details you will learn, there is the more encompassing benefit of feeling in control, of actively participating in your treatment. This, in itself, can be therapeutic.

A word of warning: Be careful about reading things that are overly technical or beyond your ability to understand clearly. When I was first diagnosed with my kidney problem, I asked my nephrologist for information about my condition. He gave me an article from a scientific journal. I read it—and became terrified at the thought that I was facing renal failure within three to five years. It turned out that certain things in the article had simply gone over my head; I didn't have the characteristics that suggested such a grim prognosis. But my overly ambitious reading gave me a nasty scare.

Take responsibility, and listen to your body. At the end of the day, you are ultimately responsible for seeing to your health. Doctors and nurses may have special expertise, but they have many people to look after; you have only one. Even more important, you are the only person who knows how it feels to live inside your body. So pay attention to what your body tells you.

Does a certain medication seem to disagree with you? If so, note the problem and be sure to tell your doctor. Does something hurt? Try to figure out exactly where the pain is and describe it as accurately as possible; pain often tells a story. Are you unnaturally tired? Don't accept fatigue as inevitable. Study it to discern patterns and causes.

If you are passive in your medical treatment, you are doing yourself a serious disservice. Do some of the thinking and some of the work. It's your life.

A final word. For those of us who are fat, our heaviness tends to be a more or less constant preoccupation, the defining factor in many different aspects of our lives. Certainly this is true in how we view our health.

Your cholesterol is high? Oh, that's because you're fat.

You're borderline diabetic? It must have to do with your weight.

In fact, these things are not so simple. There are thin diabetics and there are skinny people with high cholesterol. Without question, weight is a risk factor in these and many other ailments, but it is one risk factor among many. As foolhardy as it would be to deny the dangers of fatness to our health, it would be equally incorrect to imagine we can blame our fatness for everything that goes wrong as we age.

On the opposite side of the coin, it would be simplistic to imagine that losing weight is a cure for a given condition—or for *every* condition. Again, diseases and their treatments are more complex than that.

In general, is it healthier to be less fat? Yes. But that is not the same thing as saying that weight loss should be a universal prescription for every malady. Medical science simply doesn't know enough to make that blanket assertion. When a doctor's knee-jerk advice regarding every problem is "lose weight," chances are that conventional thinking, blind faith, and, very possibly, an antifat bias are driving his or her thinking.

Beware of treatments that claim to be the cure for everything. Remember, it wasn't so long ago that physicians felt that way about bloodletting!

CHAPTER 15

CATHARSIS . . .
AND CALM

So then, by the end of 1997 it seemed that I had both the tools and the incentive to really control my eating and manage my weight. I'd had the benefit of almost eight full years of psychotherapy. I was a regular and a veteran at the gym. I'd had a clear wake-up call regarding health issues related to my fatness. With all that going for me, I guess there was only one possible outcome: I continued getting heavier.

As 1998 began, I weighed 309 pounds and was extremely unhappy about it. I had now crossed the 300-pound threshold nine different times. Being north of it made me nervous and frustrated; my all-time high of 332 loomed dangerously close. I felt physically crummy and emotionally fragile. I was in one of those hypersensitive phases when everything seemed to revolve around my fatness—how I was perceived by others, how my own life was defined and circumscribed. By early 1998, I had decided that I would try to write this book. A friend of mine, a writer by profession, had suggested that I keep a diary registering my thoughts and feelings. While I believe this was a valuable exercise, in the near term it had the effect of making me even more preoccupied with my gloomy and sometimes self-accusing thoughts.

In early January, for instance, Carol and I flew to Minneapolis for Fritz Mondale's 70th birthday party. As we arrived, we ran into one of Mondale's closest friends, a man I hadn't seen in more than 10 years. After polite hellos, he said, "You know, I still remember the night that you and I and Fritz were out for dinner, and you ate three whole racks of ribs!" He said it with all good humor, but it made me feel awful. I duly noted in my journal that I'd met yet another person whose most vivid memory of me was an occasion when I gorged myself.

Later that same evening, a woman with whom I'd been chatting excused herself just before dessert was served. She returned moments later, bringing me an especially large piece of chocolate birthday cake. No doubt intending to be kind, she told me that the pieces being cut hadn't seemed big enough for me, so she asked to have a bigger one. Did it ever occur to her that I needed *less* cake, not more? In any case, the jumbo slice was there in front of me, so I finished every crumb.

Just a few days later, back in Washington, I was in a meeting with a good friend and colleague. After discussing the business at hand, we drifted off to other things, and I told this person about some research I was doing on my medical and diet history and how it felt to be reconstructing incidents from many years ago. I was feeling very sad as I spoke to him, and I suppose it showed. As I was leaving his office, he put an arm around my shoulder and said, "Big or small, you are always my best friend."

Now, I have always been grateful for the support and affection of my friends, but in this instance I was positively overwhelmed. I choked up immediately. By the time I reached the street I was in tears. Clearly, my nerves were raw; something was brewing. But I had no way of knowing that this episode was only a prelude to the explosive catharsis that would happen just a couple of days later.

I was in session with Bill, my psychotherapist. As was my custom, I was easing into—or perhaps avoiding—the hard work by giving Bill a general recitation of incidents and thoughts and feelings that had occurred since we'd last met. But when I came to a brief description of what had transpired with my friend, I started crying.

Over the course of my years with Bill, there had been some teary moments, but nothing like this. This was quaking and convulsive sobbing. I don't know how long it lasted—probably no more than a minute, two at most—but while I was in its grip I could no more have stopped it than I could hold back a rushing train. Through tears, I could see that Bill looked genuinely concerned. I mumbled that this was a good thing, not a bad thing, and I kept on bawling.

In that moment it seemed that everything came crashing down and flooded over me: all the defenses I'd built up, all the memories I'd swept under the carpet, all the wounds I'd shrugged off at the time but which had left scars nonetheless. In relating some of those thoughts and feelings, I need now to impose an order on them, to tell them one by one, but that isn't how I experienced them at the time. At the time I felt everything at once, in one great spasm of emotion and release.

It was as if I once again saw the faces and recalled the names of the boys who had inflicted the hurts I'd borne for nearly half a century: The boy who grabbed my breast in the junior high school shower. The "friend" who, as early as fourth grade, had nicknamed me "barrel of fudge." I was assailed by a flurry of *whys* and *what ifs*. Why had I tried so hard to play along with the teasing and the name-calling? Why had I denied the pain and tried to beat back the embarrassment? What if I'd been able to muster more awareness and more nerve and tell my tormentors that they were hurting me? Would they have stopped?

I thought about the times that I had played the jolly fat man—and I felt like a bit of a fool. Building slapstick gags around my own size. Performing crazy feats of overeating for the amazement and entertainment of other people. Why? To be liked? To publicly act out my private sense of shame?

I pictured my own body. I saw myself in fleeting but entirely unprotected glimpses, like when a reflection in a store window takes you by surprise, and you see yourself as though you were a passing stranger. The person I saw did not match the image I carried of myself. The person I saw was big and wide. That much I knew. But I'd believed that I was somehow graceful, that some of my ease on the dance floor followed me around. Now I saw a person with a tortured, rambling gait, the evidence of physical damage caused by too much weight. How many times had people asked why I was limping? Movement caused me pain; pain made me clumsy. Where was that little bit of elegance my vanity wanted to believe in?

I discovered a terrible streak of bias in myself. I didn't like the fat person I saw. It was me, and yet I wanted to believe I didn't really look that way. Not *that* big. Not *that* fat. But how could I ever accept myself if I was prey to the same prejudices that I accused the nonfat world of having?

Anger, sadness, self-pity . . . self-doubt, uncertainty, insecurity . . . The feelings flooded over me, melding into an overriding sense of frustration and failure. After all this time and all this effort, why couldn't I overcome this thing that haunted me? Why couldn't I figure out this problem? Why couldn't I finally be done with it?

Gradually, I regained my composure. The sobbing ended, my breathing returned to normal—and I felt a hell of a lot better. Not that I'd suddenly, miraculously left behind my anguish; you don't undo a lifetime's worth of struggle in a few minutes of emotional release, however dramatic that release might be.

Still, I felt unburdened and calm. And in the calm that followed the catharsis, a new feeling, a feeling of gratitude, crept in. Yes, I'd had a fair bit of pain in my life, a wearying number of setbacks, a seemingly endless pattern of progress and reversal. But for all of that, the life I'd been living was a wonderful one. Somehow, in my own pained, imperfect, and therefore human way, I had dealt with the hurdles that were put in my path.

I wasn't done with the issue of my fatness. Probably I never would be. But if I hadn't conquered my fatness, nor had I let my fatness conquer me. My fatness and I seemed to have reached a kind of stalemate, an accommodation. And I realized that was nothing to be ashamed of.

For those of us who are fat, dealing with our fatness is a challenge we face every minute of every day. To some extent, fatness is an issue in every breath we take. Every time we get up from a chair, or meet a new person, or make a food choice, or confront a crowded elevator, our size and how we feel about it must be factored in.

Because dealing with fatness is such an ongoing, moment-by-moment process, those of us who are fat aren't necessarily conscious of the tactics we use to figure out what's comfortable, what *works*. We generally rely on instinct, on half-remembered past experience. But I believe it's also helpful to keep in mind some more encompassing strategies. In reaching an accommodation with fatness, here are some things that I've found useful.

Focus on yourself. There is no such thing as "the average person." The so-called average person is a myth made up of spare parts and statistics, not a creature of flesh and blood. Yet we are constantly bombarded with so-called facts about this so-called average person: what the average person weighs, what the average person eats, how much the average person exercises, and so forth.

But the problem with this average person is that, even if he did exist, he wouldn't be living in the same world we do—a world in which each individual is unique. No two of us have the same exact metabolism, the same exact emotional make-up. Insofar as "norms" and "averages" provide a very general sense of the range of human possibilities, fine, no harm done. The problem, though, is that norms can easily become accusing and seem like desirable goals rather than neutral guidelines. For those of us who are different, the tendency is to blame ourselves for not conforming to the standard, rather than to protest that the standard clearly wasn't designed with us in mind.

My advice, then, is to forget about the average person and develop your own standards based on who you actually are. No one knows better than you what your realistic weight might be. No one can tell you how much food or exercise you need or can handle. Only you can know how you differ from others. Only you can decide what works for you, what is possible and desirable inside your own skin. Your personal reality is both unique and legitimate. Believe in it.

Inform yourself. The good news is that there is more information available than ever before on the subject of fatness—its causes, implications, and treatment, either through diet, medication, or even surgery. Unfortunately, this avalanche of information is also the bad news. There's so much information, and it changes so quickly, and so much is tainted by faddism or blatant commercial interest, that it's all but impossible for any one person to absorb it all or to separate the useful stuff from the sales pitches and the malarkey. If, like me, you tend toward the compulsive, it's awfully difficult to know when to *stop* doing research, since the torrent of information never seems to slacken.

But none of that is an excuse for remaining ignorant. As I argued in regard to medical matters, if you have an ailment, it is your responsibility to educate yourself about it; since fatness itself is a chronic disease, all of us who are afflicted with it have a responsibility to study up.

How best to do that? Of the many forms in which information is available, all have their advantages and their drawbacks.

The Internet is an astonishing resource, but remember: Anyone can post anything on the Internet. There are virtually no filters, no fact-checking, no guarantee of accuracy or reliability. Unless the information comes from a known and respected site like that of the American Heart Association or the American Diabetes Association, it should be regarded with some skepticism.

Television has plenty of coverage on matters of fatness, much of it—not counting the infomercials and the recent team weight-loss programs—responsible and serious. But TV has a built-in bias toward the trendy. What's hot this week or month? What media shrink or fat celebrity has a new book out? The information conveyed might very well be of value, but you can be pretty sure that this month's "last word" on fatness will be rewritten for next month's last word on fatness. Are carbs in or out this week? If the buzzword changes next week, is anything really different? The important question is, what does the coverage have to do with the ongoing issues of your fatness and how you deal with it?

Books cover a tremendous gamut. At one extreme are scientific tomes that may contain important research and insights but are heavy sledding for the layperson. At the other end of the spectrum is the never-ending procession of mass-market diet books. How valuable are these? I guess they must be good, since I've lost weight on every diet I've ever read about. Then again, I've always gained it back. If a diet book does nothing more than give you a new eating regimen to follow for a while, then its benefit will be fleeting. The far more significant criterion for a book is whether it helps you change the way you live.

The bottom line in all of this is that, however you prefer to get your information, *keep your critical faculties switched on*. It is a poignant truth about human nature that the more desperate people are, the more easily they are persuaded to believe in miracle cures and other nonsense. Don't let your yearning to be thinner overwhelm your common sense. If a claim sounds too good to be true, it probably is. If someone promises to make you skinny while you sleep, he's lying. If someone offers you a pill that miraculously targets belly fat, he's selling snake oil.

Test everything in the crucible of your own hard-earned insight and experience. Be skeptical. And please, bring that skepticism to bear even in the reading of this book. It is my sincere hope that the things I have to say will resonate and be of use to other fat people, as well as those who care about the fat people in their lives. But who knows? Your experience and your feelings may be quite different from mine. Just as there is no such thing as an average person, there is no such thing as an average fat person. Again, respect your own uniqueness. If my advice doesn't ring true for you, ignore it. You are the final arbiter of value.

Use your support team. "No man is an island," in the famous words of John Donne. Each of us looks to many other people for help, companionship, and affection, not to mention special expertise of various kinds. My own support team consists of my wife, other family members, and a number of close friends; it also includes my doctors, trainers, therapist, and yoga teachers. Obviously, I relate to my yoga teacher differently from how I relate to a dear old friend, and I speak with my wife differently from how I speak with my therapist. Still, there are certain general points to be made about our support teams and how we can benefit most from having them in our lives.

Every team needs a leader, and when it comes to your support team, the obvious choice is *you*. You have the most at stake. You're the only one for whom taking care of your life is a full-time occupation.

As leader, you have certain responsibilities that are common to the leadership of any team.

Make sure you have confidence in everyone whom you rely on. Encourage team members to communicate. If some don't work well together, help them solve their differences, or make a change.

Above all, let people know that their contributions are appreciated. The "job," after all, is the maintenance of your own well-being. So help people feel good about helping you feel good.

Relate to others with understanding. I didn't ask to have the disease that's kept me overweight for my entire life, and it is my firm conviction that it's not my "fault" that I am fat. At the same time, it's no one else's fault either. And I have to acknowledge that the burdens and limitations imposed by my fatness have not been mine alone to bear. They have also had an impact on those around me; the closer the relationship, the greater the impact.

Let me give a clear example. My wife loves to travel. Given her druthers, Carol would spend a lot of time globe-trotting, sightseeing, and haunting galleries and museums. For that matter, she'd also do a lot of active and adventurous things like horseback riding or snorkeling. For me, some of those pastimes would be downright impossible; others have generally been too difficult or uncomfortable to be enjoyable. Carol has accommodated my limits by doing certain activities alone or with friends; in other instances, she includes me in ways in which I am comfortable. But the net result is that, because of my fatness, Carol has done less of certain things she loves than she otherwise might have.

I try not to berate myself about this; that's seldom productive. At the same time, I think it's important for me to acknowledge—with candor, not guilt, and without getting defensive about it—that Carol has made a sacrifice. Further, I believe I should honor that sacrifice by trying to be a more considerate husband in whatever other ways I can.

The broader point is that if we want other people to be sensitive to issues relating to our fatness, we in turn should be sensitive to how our fatness affects *them*. We should be able to get outside our own skin and our own insecurities and acknowledge other points of view.

Consider, for instance, the dilemmas faced by our unfat friends. Insofar as they know us well and care about us, it is natural that they should be concerned about the physical and emotional implications of our fatness. But how much should they say? How much do we want them to say? Would we welcome honest and well-intentioned comments about our weight, or would we take offense? Would we find it a relief to be able to discuss our fatness, or do we treat it as a taboo subject? For well-meaning friends, these are treacherous waters that can be successfully navigated only if we ourselves send clear signals about what's acceptable and what's off-limits.

This is easier said than done. People who've often had their feelings hurt tend to be hypersensitive about being hurt yet again; speaking for myself, I sometimes find it difficult to distinguish a remark made with kindness from one meant to wound. It's also true that words strike us differently depending on who says them. A comment from a dear and trusted friend, even if it's something we'd rather not hear, might appear motivated by caring and concern; the same words from a mere acquaintance might seem flip and hurtful.

The key, I think, is to consider not just one's own gut reaction to a comment but the intent behind it. Trust your intuition on this. If you judge a comment to be kindly meant, try to accept it gracefully, even it carries a fleeting sting. On the other hand, there is no reason, ever, to tolerate remarks that are mean-spirited or intentionally unkind.

It's up to you to establish boundaries and let people know when they have crossed them. Usually, this can be done in a way that clears the air and actually strengthens relationships. But sometimes, sadly, a calm and honest conversation doesn't solve the problem. There are people out there who just don't get it—who are either oblivious to the pain they are causing or simply don't care about the feelings of others. Leave those people behind; you don't need them in your life.

I should caution that one can go too far in this matter of trying to see situations from the other person's point of view. If taken to extremes, this can become a trap that I myself have fallen into on more than one occasion—a trap, I believe, that fat people need to make a special effort to avoid. Everyone wants to be loved. And as we go through life, we come to understand that we are more likely to be loved if we ourselves are generous and giving and focus on what other people need. But there is such a thing as overdoing it; fat people, myself included, have been known to try too hard. To compensate for being fat, to avoid the dreaded rejection that we've come to expect, we sometimes try to be all things to all people; maybe we're too willing to drop what we're doing to listen to someone else's problems, or too ready to jettison our plans to accommodate another person's schedule.

But what if we do all that and still don't feel we are receiving as much love as we crave? That just creates yet more frustration and yearning that can most readily be soothed with food.

By all means, then, try to relate to others with understanding, but not at the cost of your own best interests, and certainly not of your self-respect.

Learn to feel good about yourself. There are things you can hide and things you can't. I have usually been able to mask the physical aches and pains connected with my fatness; some of the time, I even forget about them altogether. For better or worse, I have almost always been able to hide my emotional pain as well. It simmers somewhere in the background as I move through the professional and social aspects of my life. I generally let it show only in sessions with my therapist or in intimate conversations with my wife or a handful of dear friends.

But my size itself—the sheer fact of how much space I occupy, how my body fills my clothing or the furniture— is not something that can be hidden or ignored or pushed into the background. It's with me every moment. It's there for all to see. It's there for *me* to see. It's thrust upon me every time I see my own reflection. I can analyze this or that subtle aspect of my fatness, but when it comes to the bulk and the shape of my body, there is nothing to analyze. It's simply there, relentlessly. And this, over the years, has been a source of much unhappiness and personal dissatisfaction.

My size has made me painfully self-conscious. Sometimes, when I enter a room, I find myself playing the "body check" game. Are there other fat people in the group? Am I the only one? How much will I stand out? Am I getting "looks" as I move into the gathering?

When I see another really fat man, I catch myself wondering if I look like him and wanting to believe I don't.

Over the years, through all my efforts to lose weight, to reduce my size, I've also been making a parallel effort that I've come to see as even more important: to accept the size I am. This has not been easy, but I believe I've made real progress. Here are some things that have helped.

First, it finally got through to me that my family, friends, and colleagues care way less about my size than I do. If it's not an issue for them, why should I allow it to be such a huge and constant issue for me? If those who know me best can see past my fatness to the person that I am, why shouldn't I be able to do the same?

I've also realized that, when it comes to human shapes and sizes, diversity is the name of the game. Think about the "perfect" people who work as models or are featured in advertisements. How many folks do you know who actually look like that?

Try standing on a busy street corner for a while. You'll see an amazing and wonderful array of shapes and sizes and weights and colors passing by. People strutting and people trying to disappear. Tall people, short people; wide people, narrow people. You'll soon absorb the simple truth that there is no such thing as a single "right" body type. We live our lives, and go about our business, and look for love and happiness and peace of mind in a great variety of physical trappings. And the world would be poorer and less interesting if this were not the case.

Try to move beyond appearances in relating to those around you. If you can root out your own secret biases— and let's be honest, few of us are immune to them—you will find it that much easier to shed your anxieties about how you, in turn, appear to others.

Finally, give yourself the chance to experience your body as the source of *good* feelings, not just bad ones. Learn to appreciate the simple physical pleasures.

Let yourself float in a swimming pool or languish in a sauna. Treat yourself to a massage now and then. You'll feel better about your body if your body itself feels good.

CHAPTER 16

AT LONG LAST, LOSS

One evening in the middle of 1998, Carol and I decided to go out to a movie. Indirectly and very, very slowly, this entirely routine circumstance led toward the most successful and sustainable episode of weight control I have ever managed in my life. Here's what happened.

Because I weighed over 300 pounds at the time, and because I found theater seats to be confining and uncomfortable, it was very important to me to be seated on the aisle, where I'd be assured, at least, of some extra space on one side or the other. So I insisted on getting to the movie very early. Carol objected. The film we were going to wasn't very popular, so why rush to an empty theater?

But I pushed, and we arrived half an hour before the movie was scheduled to begin. I got my aisle seat, but sure enough, Carol was right; the auditorium stayed practically empty around us. Annoyed at this flagrant waste of time, she said to me, "You know, Mike, your whole life is being driven by your worries about comfort. The size of chairs and things like that are more important to you than the actual events." Though I don't recall the exact exchange that followed, the crux of Carol's comments was that my priorities had gotten warped; I was letting my size dictate where I went and what I did. Why didn't I do something about it?

In the moment, I felt that she was being cruel. I went quiet, as I tend to do when I'm angry or upset. Over the following days and months, however, I saw that she was right. For all my efforts at not allowing my fatness to diminish my life and my possibilities, to not let it limit me or hold me back, it did hold me back in certain ways.

I really didn't like to travel. When I did travel, my emphasis was not on broadening my horizons or learning new things but on trying to maintain complete control over my circumstances; the threat of discomfort or embarrassment was a nearly constant concern. At a theater or sports arena, the width of my seat and the placement of the armrests were more crucial to my enjoyment of the evening than the quality of the play or the ball game.

When I chose a car, the determining factor was, not styling or gas mileage or price, but how much room there'd be between my stomach and the steering wheel. Even at restaurants, my choices were dictated as much by the seating as by the food; if a restaurant had only arm-chairs that I'd have to stuff myself into, I wasn't likely to go there. If it was physically difficult to get to the men's room, that was another strike against the place.

Now, in a kinder world, a world more tolerant of di-versity in human shapes and sizes, these concerns over physical comfort needn't have seemed so daunting. The-ater seats *could* be made a little wider, after all. Airline seat belts *could* be made a little longer. There are dozens, if not hundreds, of minor alterations that could make life con-siderably pleasanter for people of size, and it is my fer-vent hope that, with the progress being made in fat acceptance and the good work being done by advocacy groups, we will begin to see those sorts of humane im-provements in the world around us. In the meantime, though, I had to try to fit my body into the world as it ac-tually is. And the fit was often an awkward one.

In the fall of 1998, Carol and I attended a performance at the concert hall of the Kennedy Center. We had the good fortune to be seated in a private box; the box had separate chairs rather than fixed seating. That was the good news. The bad news was that the chairs had arms and were rather narrow. The first time I sat down, I noticed that the chair was tight around my hips; the arms seemed to lock down around my excess flesh. Right away I got worried, preoccupied, distracted from the event we were there to see. And, as I feared, when I stood up for the first intermission, the chair came with me.

It was a horrifying reprise of my little disaster in the student lounge at law school, but this time I couldn't play it for laughs. I was 60 years old. I was in the nation's capital, surrounded by colleagues, acquaintances, people I did business with. It was not cool and not funny to have a chair stuck to my backside! Doing my best to disguise the effort, I pushed hard, straightened up, and freed myself from the furniture. One person, at least, had noted my humiliation; Carol later told me that she'd been squirming with empathy at my predicament. She also recalled that the embarrassment didn't prevent either of us from scarfing down cashew nuts and M&Ms during intermission.

I suffered through the rest of the evening. Had anyone else noticed my misadventure? Were they laughing at me, pitying me? Was I sure I could prevent it happening again? Why did there have to be so damn many standing ovations?

It is perhaps surprising that, in spite of incidents like these, I let almost another year go by before I got serious about knocking off some weight. I just seemed to be drifting. For days or weeks I'd eat carefully, and then it would get away from me again. In my journal from that period, there are references to days of "nonstop eating," to "feeling especially wide," to feeling bloated and feeling lousy. On January 2, 1999, weighing 315, I duly noted one of history's shorter-lived New Year's resolutions: "I began the day determined to get back on track and at least get below 300 pounds. That resolve lasted until about dinnertime." On January 13 I hit a near-term high of 317.

Given my physical discomfort, and given that I had health issues to consider, a good support team, and a reasonable store of knowledge about what I was up against, why wasn't I more aggressive at this juncture about trying to control my weight? The answer, I believe, is a crucially important paradox—a paradox that I mentioned at the very beginning of this book. But I want to spend a little time discussing it further, because I think it might be the key to the sustainable weight loss I seem to have finally been able to achieve.

By 1998 and 1999, I had made significant progress in

dealing with the emotional issues connected with my fatness. I'd been learning not to blame myself, not to beat myself up over things that were, and remain, well beyond the reach of everyday concepts like "willpower" and "self-control." I accepted that I had a disease. I accepted that, whatever my weight at a given time, I would always be a fat person. With this acceptance came a welcome calm, a growing level of emotional comfort. Would I have liked to be thinner? Sure. Would weighing less have been better for my health? Almost certainly. But, emotionally speaking, getting thinner was just not as big an issue as it used to be. I was okay as I was. I didn't lose weight because I didn't *need* to lose weight.

But the other side of the paradox took a while to sink in. *The fact that I didn't* need *to lose weight suggested that maybe now I could lose weight—and keep it off.*

That might seem illogical, but it's entirely true to human nature. It's tough to lose weight—or to stop smoking or quit drinking—when you're feeling desperate about it; the desperation itself pushes you back toward the behavior you're trying to avoid. But now, to a considerable degree, the pressure was off. I wasn't desperate; I wasn't frenzied; my fatness was an inconvenience but it wasn't in itself making me unhappy. I realized that I did in fact have a choice. I couldn't choose to be a thin person, but I could choose to manage my fatness better or less well.

Something basic but elusive had finally gotten through to me: *accepting a situation is not the same thing as giving up on it.* Acceptance, in fact, is probably a vital step in learning to deal with a problem most effectively.

These thoughts did not occur to me all at once or come with a flash of revelation. Rather, they ripened over time, bringing with them a readiness to make a fresh attempt at managing my weight.

Then, one day in late July of 1999, while I was on the treadmill at the gym, I announced to one of my trainers, who also worked as a dietitian, that for a period of 13 weeks I would do whatever she recommended by way of an eating regimen and weight-loss program. She seemed a bit surprised by the abruptness of my proposal and the clear commitment behind it. Frankly, I was a bit surprised myself. But what can I say? I guess I was finally ready.

A few days later I met with Kate, the trainer/dietitian, and we began to talk about the basics of my program. From the start, it was clear that there were certain refreshing differences in her approach from most of the many others I had tried.

For starters, there were to be no specific weight-loss targets—no arbitrary numbers to get obsessed about, no artificial goals to be depressed about missing. Rather, we would just agree on the initial time period of 13 weeks and do our best.

Second, there were virtually no foods that were absolutely proscribed, no forbidden fruits for which I'd build up overwhelming cravings. I was urged to cut out butter and obviously crazy things like potato chips, but other than that, the emphasis was on the elusive grail of moderation. If I wanted meat, I should try to limit it to three or four ounces a day. If I fancied sweet desserts other than fruit, I should eat reasonable portions no more than twice a week.

Third, Kate's approach was free of gimmicks and buzzwords and brought things back to basics; that is, to the question of caloric intake. As I've said before, once you get past the trends and the sales pitches and the hocus-pocus, this is what all weight-loss formulas finally come down to. If you take in more calories than you burn, you will gain weight; if you take in fewer calories than you burn, you will lose weight. Kate did urge me to be aware of the mix of protein, fat, and carbohydrate in my diet, but as a way of keeping within my calorie guidelines, not in hopes of finding some magic proportion that would mysteriously change the math.

Finally, there was nothing extreme or radical in the regimen Kate proposed for me. Before the start of the actual diet period, we did a test week, during which I recorded everything I ate. With the help of a computer program, Kate figured that my average daily intake had been 2,843 calories. She recommended that I lower that to 2,400 to 2,500—a mere 12 or 15 percent reduction. Compare that to the zero calories of my hospital fast, or the 800 calories that followed my protein-sparing regimen, or the 1,000 calories I took in at Pritikin, and it becomes clear that the goal here was not a steep and sudden weight loss but, rather, an approach that I could live with, a diet that could become part of my *diaita*.

On August 18, with no fanfare and a lot less angst than had generally accompanied the start of other diets, I began. As I would throughout, I kept careful records of what I ate and how much I exercised. During the first couple of weeks, eager for results, I actually took in fewer calories than I was "allowed." This did not seem difficult—yet. In the course of my professional life, I had the usual meetings that featured the usual bagels and cream cheese and coffee cakes and scones; it didn't cost me too much anguish to ignore them at this point.

My progress was real but undramatic. It was designed to be undramatic, as dramatic weight loss is seldom sustainable. Still, near the end of my 13-week commitment, I found myself getting a little frustrated and tense. I'd lost 23 pounds and weighed 286. I had a long way to go, and the rate of reduction was pretty slow. Would I be able to stick with it? There was only one way to find out. I re-upped for another 13 weeks.

Almost as soon as I'd made this fresh commitment, I was assailed by a bout of "diet fatigue." The things that were good for me just didn't seem appealing; but when, as the diet permitted, I treated myself to something tastier (read: fatty or sweet), I had a tough time limiting amounts. Struggling to maintain my resolve, I thought back to other instances when my commitment had waned. What had gone wrong? Generally, I'd reach some short-term goal—either a number on the scale or some improved degree of physical comfort—and my determination would begin to weaken. At the same time, other, subversive forces, seemed to get stronger. I built up more and more desire for the foods I'd been denying myself. My "fat dependence" kicked in, and I began to scare myself with the possibility of facing the world without the insulation and the commanding size that I was used to.

This time around, I at least had the advantage of understanding that process a little better. I knew that my health and comfort issues would not be solved by a small and possibly fleeting weight loss. I also had less fear of being thinner. By another one of those paradoxes that my time in therapy had helped me grasp, the fact that I was more accepting of my fatness suggested that I had less need of it; with a more clear and confident sense of who I was, I could dare to shed my armor. I tried my best to hang in there with the program.

At the end of the second 13 weeks, I'd dropped another 15 pounds and weighed in at 271. I was averaging around 2,200 calories per day, and I was beginning to notice gratifying changes in my body and how it fit into the world. I no longer needed an extender on my airline seat belt. My clothes fit more loosely, even in the waist. I signed on for another quarter of a year. Maybe the best thing was that I never seriously considered *not* continuing.

Make no mistake—the diet was still difficult, the process still a roller coaster of emotions and moods. Looking back at my journal from this time, I am struck by all the ups and downs. At times I wanted food so badly that I couldn't sit still, couldn't stop fidgeting. There were nights I worried that I'd never get to sleep without some sinful snack to take the edge off my anxiety.

But if the rigors were real, so were the rewards. I'd shed four inches around my middle. I amazed myself by feeling quite satisfied by half a cup of nonfat ice cream. Almost everything seemed easier; I felt like a weight lifter who'd moved to lighter weights. To my delight, I found that I could dance again. My knees didn't hurt, my feet didn't ache.

At the end of my third 13-week cycle, I'd lost another 16 pounds. I now weighed 255. I felt terrific, but I was facing a fresh danger: I was starting to fantasize about what might be possible. Could I get back to my wedding weight of 235 in time for our 35th anniversary in mid-August? I tried to banish the thought. Setting too-specific goals was really dangerous. If you missed the goal, you were frustrated and discouraged; if you reached it, you could easily imagine you were finished with the task. Either way, a goal could kill you. I tried my best to forget about a target and focus instead on steady progress.

When does a certain way of eating cease to be a "diet" and become simply how one lives, what one eats? Could I keep this up forever in some form? These were the things I asked myself as I set out on the cycle that would bring me up to one full year.

As I went along, the regimen became easier in some ways, more difficult in others. Because habit is such a powerful thing, healthy eating leads to healthy eating; that's what made it easier. On the other hand, as I became relatively leaner, the pace of weight loss slowed; I was more inclined to get stuck on frustrating plateaus that tested my resolve. Also, the less I weighed, the fewer calories I burned in the normal course of getting through the day; to achieve the same result, I had to keep cutting back on intake.

Still, my progress was very visible by now, and I was starting to receive a gratifying stream of compliments from friends and colleagues. I soon learned that handling a compliment graciously, like everything else, takes practice. On a couple of occasions, I made the mistake of trying to answer kind words with attempts at witty replies—saying, essentially, *Gee, how did I look to you before?* Or, *Boy, guess you thought I used to be really fat!* I soon realized that I was turning what should have been a wonderful moment into a somewhat uncomfortable situation, and I learned to keep my mouth shut or just say thank you.

One day a colleague saw me on the street and addressed me as "Your Thinness." A concierge at a hotel whose restaurant I often visited called me an inspiration. False modesty aside, this felt terrific. One day, at a social event at the White House, President Clinton himself congratulated me on my loss of weight; that was one for the scrapbook.

Things were going well. Then, in August 2000, a crisis loomed: I was heading to Los Angeles for yet another Democratic National Convention. As I've related, conventions had been my downfall; I'd been to eight so far and gained weight every time. The pressure was brutal; in the past, I'd been able to cope only by eating disastrous quantities of fattening food. Now I was looking at three weeks of nonstop stress, with every meal either in a restaurant or catered. What would happen this time?

Weighing myself daily was an important part of my regimen. While many hotels have scales in their bathrooms, they are notoriously unreliable. So I ordered a good scale from a favorite catalog and had it shipped to my hotel. When Carol came out to stay with me for the days leading up to the convention itself, she admitted feeling a great sense of relief upon seeing that scale; it struck her as visible evidence that I was serious about sticking with my routine, that I wasn't letting the convention serve as a pretext for having things go to hell.

It so happened that our 35th wedding anniversary took place in the midst of that convention. And I think it's emblematic of what a happy time it was, how good we felt about each other and ourselves, that Carol joined me on the podium to accept a bouquet and have our anniversary announced over the enormous P.A. system. It wasn't a televised moment; most delegates were probably busy with other things; still, it was a time when we stood up in a very public setting and proudly said, *Here we are.*

I got through the convention period with no appreciable weight gain. Honestly, I didn't find it that difficult.

By coincidence, the day I flew back to Washington was also my one-year anniversary on this diet. I weighed 239 pounds; a year before, I'd been at 309. My waist size was 48 inches, down from 56. Once again I faced the question of quitting or continuing. I chose to continue. Partly, this was due to fear. I'd never been good at holding steady at a given weight; I was concerned that if I stopped losing, I would soon begin to gain. Mainly, though, I continued because I liked the way it felt. The weight loss itself was satisfying, but there was the further issue of what the weight loss represented—a private but profound sense of victory. Tentatively, at least, I was mastering something that had always threatened to master me.

Early in year two, I began to grapple with a time lag in my self-image; I had flashes of something like an out-of-body experience. I didn't quite recognize myself. Consciously, I knew I'd gotten thinner, but I often felt like I was a fat person looking at this thinner person as if he were somebody else. While it was nice to be reminded of how much smaller I'd become, this image confusion was not entirely pleasant; a certain anxiety went with it. In losing so much weight, even though God knows I wanted to, I was losing part of who I was, letting go of something I had always *used*. Was I really ready to go forward in my life without it?

For a while I seemed stuck between two fears—the fear of gaining back the weight I'd lost and the fear of losing too much of myself. Perhaps for that reason, over the next six months or so, my weight basically went nowhere. In my fifth quarter-year of the diet, I lost a mere four pounds; over the 13 weeks that followed, I actually gained two pounds, winding up at 237. Was fat dependence preventing me from losing more?

Or was there perhaps a more positive way of looking at my long stay at this plateau? Maybe my regimen was making the subtle shift from weight loss to weight management. To put it another way, maybe I was no longer "on a diet." Maybe I was following a long-term framework that helped me to control my eating.

I still needed help. I was food-dependent; food was still my drug of choice, and I looked to it for comfort, for stress reduction, to reward myself. I still had the damnedest time resisting fattening food if it was put in front of me. I still found it all but impossible to eat a little bit of something if there was more to be had. How many times had I made the mistake of imagining I could eat a single French fry, a small taste of chocolate cake?

When it came to food, I'd always been compulsive; that tendency hadn't gone away. I'd always been an overeater, and I was an overeater still. The difference, though, was this: I was now an overeater who only very rarely overate.

In the spring of 2001, as I neared a year and three-quarters on my program, I started losing weight again. I think it was at least partly due to an uptick in both the frequency and intensity of my workouts at the gym. I'd been establishing an encouraging and healthy cycle. As I lost more weight, my general fitness improved; as I grew more fit, I could work out harder and burn more calories, which kept me losing weight.

But my progress consisted of more than pounds alone; I also felt stronger and more vigorous. Around this time I began to notice strange swellings in my upper arms—biceps! I guess they'd been there all along, but I'd never been able to locate them before. One day, as I did an exercise with my legs up in the air, the trainer informed me that my thighs were disappearing.

By early summer, I'd broken through the barrier of 230. Then, one day, I found myself shopping at one of my favorite stores: the Chocolate Moose, purveyors of the chocolate almond bark I loved so much and that I often used to binge on. Walking past the counter, I felt the old familiar tug that told me I would not be able to resist. And I didn't. I ordered three ounces of the delicacy—a far cry from the two pounds or more I used to eat at a sitting—and I duly recorded the calories in my notebook. In my own mind, at least, being able to have this small amount, and be satisfied, and stop, was a more important step than being able to deny myself the candy altogether.

On August 15, Carol and I celebrated our 36th wedding anniversary. I weighed 225 pounds—10 pounds less than on our wedding day. You may recall that I'd flirted with the idea of trying to reach my wedding-day weight for our *35th* anniversary. Well, I missed it by a year, but so what? As in a Zen story, I finally hit the target by learning to forget the target.

A few days later, I completed my second year of following this regimen. *Two full years.* It sounds like a long time, and I suppose it was. But time passes, regardless of what we do, or don't do; the same 2 years would have gone by whether I was managing my weight or not. Two years earlier, I'd weighed 309; my legs hurt, I was often short of breath, and I couldn't dance. Now, if you believed the calendar, I was 2 years older, yet I felt way more youthful and spry. I'd shed 84 pounds. Some of the time I'd been uncomfortably hungry; there's no denying it. At moments I'd felt the addict's itching desperation for a fix. But it was no surprise that weight control was difficult; if I knew anything at all, I knew that. The surprise was that in this instance it had turned out to be possible.

I had no thought of giving up the program that had by now become a part of my routine. I counted calories, limited fat, kept records of my eating and my workouts. The weight continued to come off—very slowly, but that was fine. I'd come to be a firm believer in the virtue of the gradual.

In late October, weighing 221, I sat in my therapist's office, fumbling for a way to get the session started. As he often did, Bill asked me what I was really thinking. So I told him: "I seem to have nothing to say. Life is awfully good. I've lost weight, and it seems to be staying off. I'm just making up things to talk about."

Bill said, "I know. You're done."

"Done?" I echoed, in what was probably a somewhat strangled tone of voice. Done. The concept, after all these years, was just so strange.

"Yes," he said, and smiled.

I knew he was right. In fact, for the past several months I'd been feeling that there was little left for Bill and me to do together. I'd learned a lot about why I'd become fat, and food dependent, and fat dependent. To the extent that I could work through my problems and beat them back, I believe I'd done so. I don't kid myself that I'd unearthed and tackled everything, or even that I'd tackled everything that had been unearthed; some of it was just too difficult, and I was not prepared to face the work and pain of dealing with the issues that still remained. Suffice it to say that we'd tackled everything that I was willing to delve into, and that was good enough. I'm not sure human beings ever quite get to the bottom of knowing why they are the way they are, and maybe that's a mercy.

In any case, I was now ready to move on. At my request, Bill and I had a couple more sessions, mainly to talk about my plans to write this book. Then, with the somewhat dizzying abruptness that always goes with the end of something, my therapy was over.

This happened just before I reached 2¼ years of successful weight control and seemed to correspond with a sort of personal renaissance. Getting comfortable with my lower weight and smaller body opened me up to other sorts of changes as well. Later that autumn I shaved off the mustache I'd had, with only one brief interruption, for 40 years. The mustache, in some small way, had been one of the things I used to make myself memorable and imposing; rather suddenly I didn't seem to need it anymore.

Barely a week after shedding my facial hair, I changed the style of my eyeglasses. For a quarter century I'd favored dark and heavy frames, frames that were distinctive if not exactly beautiful, that seemed to belong on a fat man with a big bald head. Now I went for something much lighter that showed more of my face. In ways both literal and symbolic, I was coming out of hiding, letting the world see more of me than I had for decades.

The new year came, and I continued with my regimen. In January of 2002, Carol and I found ourselves at the

Kennedy Center once again, sitting in the same box where I'd had my humiliating scuffle with the furniture a few years before. This time I sat quite comfortably in my armchair. When the time came to stand for an ovation, I fought the impulse to hold the chair down with my hands and make a preemptive strike against the threat of getting stuck. I needed to see what would happen if I just stood up. Well, nothing happened. I rose to my feet, unrestricted, and joined in the applause.

I thought often in those months about Bill's comment that I was "done." In some ways it was true, and in other ways, of course, it wasn't. I was finished with my therapy, with the most rigorous and systematic phase of soul-searching and the most intimate sort of education. But I wasn't finished with my fatness or the struggles it entailed. In my heart I knew that. I'd worked on my awareness and on changing some of my behaviors, but I was still the person I'd been for nearly 63 years now. For me, temptation would always be there; the world remained full of stress and chocolate. My tendencies were still my tendencies; compulsion could assert itself at any moment.

Neither the calendar nor the scale could tell me when I'd done enough, when I was beyond the danger of gaining weight again, when I'd reached an end point.

There *was* no end point—and that was a difficult but very useful realization.

I was no longer "on a diet"; I was living my life as best I could. To put it another way, I wasn't merely working on my weight, I was working on *myself*—trying to be happy, trying to be healthy, trying to hold on to peace of mind.

Goals and targets really were beside the point; acceptance and well-being are not sold by the pound. What mattered was how I lived and how I felt from day to day. I seemed to have found a *diaita* that worked for me. The challenge now—the adventure—was in seeing if I could stick with it.

EPILOGUE

IF YOU WANT TO LOSE WEIGHT

I have tried to tell this story honestly, and honest stories seldom have neat and simple endings or completely happy ones. I wish I could say that the success I enjoyed in managing my fatness from 1999 to early 2002 marked a final victory—that I never again allowed my eating to get out of control, that my weight never again traced out the yo-yo pattern that has dogged me all my life. The truth, unfortunately, isn't quite so tidy.

In April 2002, although I was still following the regimen I'd been on for more than 2½ years, I had a meeting with a new nutritionist. In retrospect, this was already a sign of looming trouble. Why would I flirt with a new weight-control program unless my commitment to the existing program was waning? Why fiddle with something that had worked so well?

Sure enough, through the spring and summer, it became clear that my resolve was beginning to let go. The backsliding was subtle and gradual. Most days my eating was okay; most weeks I fulfilled my workout schedule. But my lapses became a bit more frequent, a little more extreme. I recalled the uncomfortable, almost sick feeling that went with a serious bout of overeating. By September my weight was back up to 239.

The gain itself wasn't terribly significant, but I was upset and frightened by the trend; I'd been through this too many times before. This time I was determined to arrest the upward spiral before it took on too much momentum. I spoke with my doctor about the possibility of getting back on a modified protein-sparing fast. For six weeks, I once again lived on yogurt and protein packets, augmented only by some simple vegetables. The pounds melted away; by mid-November I was down to 219.

But if I'd learned anything during the long, slow but successful period of weight control that began in 1999, it was this: if the object was a sustainable loss, then gradual was better. Weight that came flying off tended just to fly back on. I started to gain again as soon as the protein-sparing fast was over, and by April 9, 2003, my 64th birthday, I'd yo-yoed back up to 243. My clothes were starting to feel snug across the middle. Exercise was once again becoming more of an effort and more of a chore. By early 2004, I was back above 250. That September, I began yet another protein-sparing fast but never dipped lower than 239, which I hit on my 65th birthday; at this writing, in fall 2005, I weigh 235. My weight seems to have settled into a quite narrow range—and I'm not sure if this is the good news or the bad news. I looked and felt better at 220. At the same time, I vividly remember the discomfort and self-consciousness I felt at 300 or 332; if I can continue to avoid revisiting those highs, I'll be enormously relieved.

But why have I landed so solidly in this tight range? Is 235 or 250 somehow the "right" weight for me, my own personal norm? Who's to say? You won't find it in a government bulletin or on a doctor's office chart. But is there something in my body itself, in my physiology—a set point, as it is sometimes called—that is keeping me pegged right where I am? Science can't yet answer that one, but I prefer to think that my current weight is not inevitable. In spite of all the limits that real life places on our freedom, I continue to believe I can be thinner; I can accept my situation without giving up on doing better. The struggle is renewed each morning.

Throughout this book I have taken the position that, for those of us who've been quite fat from an early age, fatness may be a matter of degrees, but it is not, finally, a matter of choice; it is not a consequence of things that can be changed by "discipline" or "willpower." Rather, it's a complicated challenge—a disease, in my view—that affects our lives in many different ways and that needs to be managed.

For some people, "managing fatness" means nothing more than trying to lose weight. But, in fact, losing weight is only one aspect of dealing with the reality of being a fat person—and not necessarily even the most important one. Managing fatness means accepting ourselves as who we are. It means finding our way, socially and professionally, in a world not always sensitive to our needs and feelings. It means trying to stay as healthy and fit as possible, in spite of the risks and limitations our excess weight imposes.

Managing fatness, in short, means learning to live a full and satisfying life at whatever weight and size we happen to be. As I've argued from the outset, it is not the goal of life to be thin; the goal of life is to be happy and fulfilled.

As far as weight loss goes, there are various ways of managing it. One of those ways is simply not to bother: forget the scale, forget dieting, eat what you feel like, and let your fatness take you where it will. I personally would not recommend this strategy, but I do not disrespect it either. Trying to lose weight, or not trying to, is a matter of personal choice. Societal pressures may be powerful, but that doesn't mean that they are right or fair. No one else can tell you how you *ought* to eat or what you *ought* to weigh. It's your life. Whatever your current weight is, if you're at peace with it—if you're comfortable emotionally and have made informed judgments about issues of health and functionality—then I say more power to you.

In my experience, though, it seems that the great majority of fat people would prefer to be at least a little lighter, a little thinner. That's certainly been the story of *my* life. So I'd like to offer some straightforward, practical advice that I hope other fat people will find helpful when—and if—they feel ready to lose weight. I offer no quick fixes or easy solutions, and what I have to say is, for the most part, based on what I've learned by sometimes frustrating trial and error. Much of it is neither more nor less than simple common sense. But that's okay; in an area where there is so much hype and emotion that can cloud clear thinking, maybe common sense is the most helpful thing of all.

Have a plan. If losing weight were simply a matter of deciding to, then any of us could awaken on any morning, randomly pick any popular diet or commercial weight-loss program, and start right in. And in fact, if your objective is nothing more than modest and temporary weight reduction, that helter-skelter approach might be good enough. Almost any diet will work *for a while*, as long as it recognizes the one immutable rule of weight control: if you want to lose weight, you must take in fewer calories than you burn.

But if your aim is a more durable, sustainable weight loss, then it helps to have a plan. You need to figure out what is likely to work *for you*. To do this, you have to give thought to some potentially painful but important questions.

Why is it important to you to lose weight at this particular time? What is your emotional state? Are you happy? Are you anxious? Will your frame of mind be a help or a hindrance in your efforts? Are there emotional issues you could or should be working on *parallel* to your work on the weight itself?

Think about your diet history. What regimens have you tried in the past? What worked and what didn't? What aspects of various programs seemed a good fit with your lifestyle and preferences, and which did not? Don't undermine your chances by choosing a program that's fundamentally at odds with your tastes and your routines.

Be responsible. If your chosen regimen involves fundamental changes in your eating style (as do, for example, the Ornish or Atkins diets), or if it is based on anything more radical than a moderate reduction in your caloric intake, consult with your doctor before starting.

Think ahead. What will happen when a particular weight-loss program has run its course? How will you maintain your new, lower weight? How will you avoid slipping back into old, counterproductive habits?

Don't just *follow* a diet; *learn* from a diet. Think about the logic and the science behind it. Regard any given program as an opportunity to add to what you know about nutrition and health and about how your own body reacts to different ways of eating. This knowledge will help you eat more wisely even after a particular program has ended.

Set goals . . . or don't. It seems to be human nature to aim at targets, to stretch toward finish lines. Our culture encourages us to be goal oriented, and some people are clearly more motivated when they have a particular objective to shoot for. But, as I discussed in the previous chapter, goals have dangers too. A missed goal is discouraging; a goal achieved can create the dangerous illusion that the job of weight control is finished. During my longest period of successful weight management, I found it helpful and liberating *not* to have a target—just to do my best from day to day and month to month.

Bottom line: This business of goals is highly individual, and you need to figure out which approach works best for you. But if you do set goals, make sure they are reasonable. Don't pledge to lose a hundred pounds before you've even dropped 10. And when you think about a final target weight, don't get carried away by what you *wish* could be. Aim for a weight that is feasible and that you'll be able to defend over time, and understand that this may never conform to your "ideal" weight according to the charts.

Keep records. I know, I know—I'm compulsive. But I happen to be a firm believer in keeping records of my weight-control efforts, and it so happens that various studies back me up about how valuable this is. Keeping records accomplishes at least three things: it provides an immediate reward each time you make an entry that shows that you are sticking with your program; it forces you honestly to confront those inevitable instances when you *don't* stick to your program; and, perhaps most useful of all, it helps to identify patterns that, if unchecked, could undermine you over time.

Say you are inclined to snack at night. Is this an occasional and relatively harmless lapse or a recurring theme that needs to be addressed? Maybe on certain days you're more likely to skip exercise; is there a common feature to these days? Keeping records is a good way to connect the dots, to see the patterns in what might otherwise seem to be random actions. Remember, it's patterns of behavior, and not just isolated instances of overeating, that tend to keep us fat.

As for how you keep your records, it really doesn't matter. Find a format and level of detail that seem logical and manageable for you. It might be useful to jot down everything you eat, along with the approximate caloric content; then again, if you carefully follow a well-tested diet program, much of the calorie counting has already been done for you. Whatever you decide to write down, do it as soon as possible after eating; it's easy to forget. Cluster the foods you have at the same time, and if the eating takes place outside the usual pattern of meals, note that as well. You should also write down the content and duration of your exercise.

Assess your progress. Recording your intake and workouts is one aspect of monitoring your program; the other side is assessing your actual results. The usual way of doing this, of course, is by getting on the scale and keeping track of your changing weight.

Now, a case could be made that the scale is both the best and worst invention of all time. On the plus side, it is completely unbiased and objective; it never kids and never lies. On the minus side, the scale can be both tyrannical and fickle. It tends to present itself as the sole measure of success or failure; its cold exactness allows for no discussion. And sometimes the scale seems to punish us even when we're following our regimen—when, for no apparent reason, we mysteriously stop losing weight or even gain a pound or two. This seems horribly unfair and can really be disheartening. For that reason, I would caution against using the scale as the *only* way of assessing your progress.

In managing fatness, pounds are not the sole consideration. Your emotional comfort and general well-being matter even more. Especially when you're at a plateau and weight loss seems to stall, it's helpful to have other, more personal ways of assessing how you're doing. Do your clothes fit differently? Are you feeling stronger? Has your stamina improved? How about your blood pressure and cholesterol? Are people noticing the change in your appearance? Are you sleeping better? All of these are valid ways of measuring your progress; all of them can help you stay motivated.

Know the pluses and minuses of your method. There is basically just one way to gain weight: take in more calories than you burn. Yet there are hundreds of variations on the theme of how to take weight off again. All have advantages and disadvantages; you'll have a better chance of making progress if you choose a method in line with your objective and your temperament.

Let me mention briefly a couple of methods that I personally have chosen *not* to try: "diet pills," prescription or otherwise, and surgery.

I've avoided diet pills for a couple of reasons. As a matter of personal preference, I don't like to take any more medication than is absolutely necessary, and I already take half a dozen different drugs for various conditions. The history of diet pills also urges caution. From thyroid supplements to amphetamines to fen-phen to ephedra, a pattern emerges. Over time, the weight-loss efficacy of each new "advance" is revised downward, while the dangers of side effects are revised upward. And a careful reading of the fine print on the labels inevitably reveals an acknowledgment that the pills work best alongside a calorie-restricted eating regimen. In other words, the pills will help you lose weight if your diet is such that you'd lose weight anyway.

That said, much research is being done and new drugs are being developed all the time. There may come a day when a diet pill is proven truly useful and safe. As of now, there are a couple of prescription drugs that appear to be of modest help in losing weight, though their greater value may be in helping to maintain a given weight. The fact is, though, that they haven't been in use long enough to know for sure.

Surgery is even more radical, and while it may make sense for certain people in certain situations, it should be considered only with utmost caution. Today's operation of choice, bariatric surgery, gets results—there's no denying that. But at what cost? A tiny fraction of patients die on the table or during recovery. A more significant percentage require additional procedures to deal with complications. Some end up with nutritional deficiencies; some experience emotional fallout, including serious depression. The potential for longer-term consequences remains to be seen.

This raises the most serious of questions: Are you willing to assume the risks for a chance at being thinner? Is your fatness making you that unhappy? For me, the answer has been no. When I considered surgery several decades ago, it did not take me long to decide that the risks were too great. However, I'm not honestly sure that my decision would be the same today, given the current state of the art.

If you decide to consider this remedy, be sure to find out your surgeon's level of experience with this particular procedure. Look for a doctor with hundreds of successful operations to his or her credit. Make sure you are in a program that includes rigorous counseling before surgery, as well as ongoing and extensive physical and psychological follow-up.

The many weight-loss methods that I have employed range from the very extreme (the zero-calorie hospital fast), to the quite extreme (the protein-sparing fast), to the somewhat extreme (Pritikin), to the very gradual (the program designed for me in 1999). These approaches were all based on the bedrock goal of reducing calorie consumption; in addition, they all featured exercise components. But they had significant differences as well.

For fast results, a more dramatic regimen has obvious advantages. But there are potential drawbacks too. On very low-calorie regimens, you are likely to lose not just fat but also muscle; it's crucial to engage in appropriate levels of exercise to avoid that outcome. Also, when your body recognizes that it is being deprived or starved, your metabolism slows down. You burn fewer calories for the same level of activity, and it takes a while to come up to speed once you resume a more normal life. After a few days on a fast, you will likely stop feeling hungry; but when the fast is over, you need to be aware of the potential for feeling *very* hungry. Trust me on this!

Generally speaking, the more radical a weight-loss regimen is, the farther it takes you from a routine that you can live with longer term. No one gets by on protein packets and fat-free yogurt or fat-free milk forever. Weight-reduction regimens end, and life goes on; one of the really crucial aspects of ongoing weight management is handling the transition *out* of weight-loss mode and into maintenance mode—getting back to how you actually eat and how you live your life. This, finally, is the best argument for a more gradual method for taking off weight—it lets you ease back into a "normal" way of eating, rather than having to reinvent your whole routine.

Maintain, maintain, maintain. Losing weight is relatively easy; keeping weight off is really difficult. We all know this; but why should it be? Viewed from a certain angle, the opposite should be true. Losing weight, after all, requires that we take in *fewer* calories than we burn; maintenance allows us about as many as we burn. Why isn't that easier to do?

The difficulty, I think, comes down to this: losing weight is a project; maintaining the loss is a career.

Losing weight requires a spurt of effort and focus that it is achievable, in part, because we know it will be temporary; maintaining the loss calls for the kind of long and patient concentration that really becomes a part of who we are and how we function. To maintain ourselves at a lower weight, we have to make some fundamental changes in how we eat and how we live. We have to break the patterns of behavior that made us fat in the first place.

Easier said than done, of course. There are powerful forces arrayed against us. If we are food dependent, we will still be tempted to turn to eating for comfort and to calm ourselves. If we are fat dependent, the weight loss itself might make us uneasy in ways we're not even conscious of.

Until those underlying issues are resolved, it's difficult to leave behind old habits. As someone whose weight has yo-yoed up and down for decades, I can testify to that.

Still, I refuse to be gloomy or defeatist about the possibility of maintaining my weight within a range that I'll feel good about, if that is what I choose to do. I've learned some things that I believe can help.

One of these is simply paying attention. We tend to be pretty vigilant when we're "on a diet." The rest of the time, though, it's easy to get careless; and when we get careless, extra calories—needless calories—slip in. There are lots of foods out there that contain way too many calories for the amount of nutrition they provide. Sugary soft drinks . . . oversize bagels—beware! And don't kid yourself that you're out of danger if you avoid the butter or the cream cheese; the bagel itself might be 300 calories. Consuming even 100 calories more than you burn each day will translate into a weight gain of 10 pounds in a year.

Be aware, as well, of the hidden calories tucked away in supposedly virtuous choices. How much cream and sugar is in that innocent-looking coffee drink? How much oil is in the dressing of that presumably healthy salad?

Paying attention also applies to what I think of as unconscious eating. Eating should be a pleasure, not a tic, but for those of us who are accustomed to turning to food to, say, relieve loneliness or alleviate boredom, it's all too easy to eat almost without noticing it. In those situations, eating is really a form of fidgeting; it has little to do with actually *enjoying* the food and is therefore a waste both of the food itself and of the extra calories. If you eat only when you intend to eat, and if you take the time and trouble to really savor what you're eating, you will probably eat less and enjoy it more.

I said at the outset of this section that a fair proportion of what I have to pass along is simple common sense. Here's some of it.

Part of maintaining a given weight is controlling the size of the portions you eat. So why not eat from smaller plates and smaller bowls? If you choose to eat ice cream, have it with a tiny spoon.

Liquids will make you feel almost as full as solid foods. Drink water or other no-calorie beverages before and during your meal.

Don't stop doing the things that have worked. If exercise and record-keeping were significant aids in helping you lose weight, keep them in the mix, even if in a less intense form, as you settle in to maintain your new size.

Another thing: I think it really helps to approach the unending task of maintaining a healthy weight with a kind of open-eyed humility. Face it—it's a hard and unrelenting job, and we are only human. We get tired. We get careless. We are prey to tendencies and pressures that we cannot fully understand, let alone master. Like all people, fat or thin, we get hungry several times each day. Appetite is the most natural thing in the world, and yet, for those of us who have the fat disease, it is the enemy.

Given the difficulty of what we're up against, it's perfectly okay to ask for help and support from spouses, friends, and colleagues. Let people know what you're trying to accomplish and what you need to do—and not do—to achieve your aim. At the very least, the people you are close to should be sensitive enough not to put extra temptation in your path. In our home, if Carol wants to keep a food that is a danger to me, she hides it. It's an innocent game, and no harm done.

If you have issues with food, don't put too much temptation in your own path. Being "strong" is an interesting concept, but whom are you trying to impress? Again, a realistic humility can help. There's no shame in admitting that you simply can't resist the chocolate in the cupboard;

if that's the case, then don't keep candy in the house. Keeping temptation out of reach can be particularly difficult when you live with one or more other people; try to work together to balance different needs and preferences. Just as there are limits to our self-control, there are also limits to our understanding. Say you pass a fast-food place on your drive home from work. Twice a week you stop there for fries. You don't want to do this; you don't mean to do this; you don't know why it happens. Well, you know what? It doesn't matter if you know why. Take a different route home from work! Insight is nice, but what counts is what we *do*. If we can modify our behavior, with or without a leap in understanding, that's plenty good enough.

Finally—not just to maintain a given weight but to get through the day with some semblance of serenity—we need to accept ourselves with all our imperfections. Perfection is not a human trait. Everyone has goof-off days; everyone messes up occasionally. If you are prone to overeating, you will overeat sometimes. If exercise, for you, is a matter of considered obligation rather than enjoyment, there will be times when you will skip your workout. No one avoids these lapses altogether, so you may as well lose the guilt and let yourself enjoy them . . . and then get back to business. The truth is, little lapses don't matter very much; you've got a lifetime to undo the tiny damage that is done. What counts is your continuing resolve.

So there it is—some of what I've lived through as a fat person, and some of what I've learned.

As this book is being completed, I am 66 years old. I have been a fat person since . . . when? Since birth? Since my first nighttime foray to scavenge food from my family's kitchen? Since the first time I was called names at school and comforted myself with candy? However you reckon it, it's been a long time to live with a disease.

A pessimist might see failure in my inability to "cure" myself through the course of all those years and all the things that I have tried. I see it differently. As I look at it, I have been engaged in a lifelong contest against a strong and tireless adversary. I've neither "won" nor "lost" the battle and never will, but I certainly have been shaped by it.

From childhood on, my fatness seemed to block the way to certain things but steer me on toward others. Denied the easy popularity that appeared to go with being trim and athletic, I needed to find other ways to have a social life, to make myself appreciated. I learned to be helpful in the background. If I couldn't be a track star, I could man the stopwatch and carry the clipboard. If I was too self-conscious to run for class president, I was quite at ease helping someone else get elected. Thus began my lifelong love of politics—a field in which I've had the good fortune to be judged not by my size but by my skills and capacity for work.

Similarly, if my fatness forced me to the sidelines of the dating game, it gave me other ways to relate to girls—and, later, women. I learned to listen. I learned the value of speaking openly about my feelings. I absorbed the trust that comes only with difficulty in matters of romance, but much more readily in friendship. I learned to be a confidante, a pal, and this has proven to be extremely valuable not only in terms of my grown-up friendships but also in my marriage. Carol and I have not been together for more than 40 years on the grounds of mere physical attraction. We are together because we share values, because we enjoy each other: because we are friends; because we love each other.

I don't kid myself that everything about my fatness has had such happy compensations. Diseases aren't picnics, after all, and some of what I've been through has been pretty miserable. I know that I've missed out on certain things. For all my love of food, it has been a long time since I simply savored a meal without fretting in some way about the consequences. I've never known the joy of the natural athlete just doing something that comes easily. I've never felt the unexamined confidence that I imagine a lean and handsome man feels when he walks into a room.

But that's okay. No life is perfect; all lives have their difficulties. At least, in the case of my fatness, I've had plenty of time to learn what I am up against, to learn what it takes to manage it, and to accept the fact that I'll be up against it forever. My weight may vary, but my fatness isn't going to go away. Where could it go? It isn't something that exists outside of me; it's part of who I am.

Would my life have been easier without my fatness? Almost certainly. Would a different life inside a different body have been better? That's impossible to say, and anyway, it doesn't matter. We don't live different lives; we live the life that we've been given. I enjoy mine, challenges and all.

ACKNOWLEDGMENTS

Sitting down to thank the people who helped to make this book possible is a daunting task.

My wife, Carol Berman, has to head the list. She was my first editor, reading each chapter and providing critical commentary on everything from punctuation to the clarity of ideas. Even more important, she allowed me to share incidents and thoughts in which we both were involved. In deference to Carol's privacy, it was understood that she could strike anything she did not want readers to see. She never invoked that privilege. And then she agreed to contribute thoughts that she had not even shared with me.

Robert Barnett is an extraordinary lawyer and authors' representative. More important to me, he is my friend. Without his guidance and publishing expertise, this book would not exist.

In 1998–99, when I first thought seriously about this project, I spoke with several published authors. They suggested that I write a proposal and a chapter or two, then begin approaching publishers. Bob advised me otherwise, urging me to write a complete first draft. In hindsight, I realize that he knew two things. One: just how difficult it was going to be for me to get comfortable sharing my story; two: how long it would take me to write a book. When a draft was finally completed and the rejection letters starting piling up, Bob never flagged in his support.

I am convinced that it was only her regard for Bob that led Stephanie Tade, then of Rodale Books, to take the time to meet with me; yet once we'd met, Stephanie became an invaluable ally. For her faith in the idea of a fat man writing candidly about his life and struggles, I am more appreciative than I can express. I am grateful, as well, for Stephanie's blend of realism and tact in advising me that my story would benefit from the involvement of a seasoned writer. She suggested Laurence Shames, and sent along a book he had written, with the late Peter Barton, called *Not Fade Away*. As luck would have it, I'd known Peter Barton, not well but well enough to recognize his voice; as I read that book I could hear Peter.

I called Larry, and thus began a slightly odd but wonderful working relationship. Over the following months, Larry came to know more about my life as a fat man than any person other than Carol or my therapist. Yet we never met until after the whole book was written. We communicated by telephone and Internet. Larry rewrote, combined, added insight and texture—but still I could see my words and phrases and thoughts. I felt very comfortable that he was telling the story I wanted told in a more compelling way than I was able to do for myself. My gratitude and affection know no bounds.

At Rodale, Chris Potash took on the task of shepherding the manuscript through the editing process. His hard work and his judicious pushing and pulling made this a better book. My thanks to him, as well as the rest of the editorial team.

Over the years, I have been lucky in having the care of a terrific group of health professionals, all of whom have shared a willingness to answer questions and to help me understand the implications of my fatness. There are three who have been particularly helpful: Dr. Arthur Frank, Dr. Jim Ramey, and Bill Picon, PhD.

The trainers at One to One, the fitness center that I found at the age of 52, gave me the gift of learning how to make exercise a part of my life. My particular thanks go to Kate Parker and Julie Ewen.

Beth Donovan is the only person other than Carol and Larry who read the entirety of my draft manuscript. She provided invaluable insights as the first person to read it from a totally neutral perspective.

The numbers of my friends who provided encouragement and help are too many to list, in part because I would certainly forget someone. But three of them—Rita Braver, Bill Harris, and Peter Hart—were particularly supportive.

Four young interns in our office—Emily Picon, Laura Simoloaris, Francesca Monga, and Beth Morrison—provided invaluable help with research and cataloguing hundreds of articles and books.

To all of the above, I say thank you.